PROJECT MANAGEMENT INSTITUTE

THE STANDARD FOR PORTFOLIO MANAGEMENT – THIRD EDITION

Library of Congress Cataloging-in-Publication Data

The standard for portfolio management / Project Management Institute. — 3rd ed.
    p. cm.
 Includes bibliographical references and index.
 ISBN 978-1-935589-69-3 (pbk. : alk. paper)
1. Project management—Standards. I. Project Management Institute.
 HD69.P75S735 2013
 658.4'04—dc23

                                                         2012046084

ISBN: 978-1-935589-69-3

Published by: Project Management Institute, Inc.
                   14 Campus Boulevard
                   Newtown Square, Pennsylvania 19073-3299 USA
                   Phone: +610-356-4600
                   Fax: +610-356-4647
                   Email: customercare@pmi.org
                   Internet: www.PMI.org

PMI Publications welcomes corrections and comments on its books. Please feel free to send comments on typographical, formatting, or other errors. Simply make a copy of the relevant page of the book, mark the error, and send it to: Book Editor, PMI Publications, 14 Campus Boulevard, Newtown Square, PA 19073-3299 USA.

To inquire about discounts for resale or educational purposes, please contact the PMI Book Service Center.
                   PMI Book Service Center
                   P.O. Box 932683, Atlanta, GA 31193-2683 USA
                   Phone: 1-866-276-4764 (within the U.S. or Canada) or +1-770-280-4129 (globally)
                   Fax: +1-770-280-4113
                   Email: info@bookorders.pmi.org

The paper used in this book complies with the Permanent Paper Standard issued by the National Information Standards Organization (Z39.48—1984).

10 9 8 7 6 5 4 3 2 1

NOTICE

The Project Management Institute, Inc. (PMI) standards and guideline publications, of which the document contained herein is one, are developed through a voluntary consensus standards development process. This process brings together volunteers and/or seeks out the views of persons who have an interest in the topic covered by this publication. While PMI administers the process and establishes rules to promote fairness in the development of consensus, it does not write the document and it does not independently test, evaluate, or verify the accuracy or completeness of any information or the soundness of any judgments contained in its standards and guideline publications.

PMI disclaims liability for any personal injury, property or other damages of any nature whatsoever, whether special, indirect, consequential or compensatory, directly or indirectly resulting from the publication, use of application, or reliance on this document. PMI disclaims and makes no guaranty or warranty, expressed or implied, as to the accuracy or completeness of any information published herein, and disclaims and makes no warranty that the information in this document will fulfill any of your particular purposes or needs. PMI does not undertake to guarantee the performance of any individual manufacturer or seller's products or services by virtue of this standard or guide.

In publishing and making this document available, PMI is not undertaking to render professional or other services for or on behalf of any person or entity, nor is PMI undertaking to perform any duty owed by any person or entity to someone else. Anyone using this document should rely on his or her own independent judgment or, as appropriate, seek the advice of a competent professional in determining the exercise of reasonable care in any given circumstances. Information and other standards on the topic covered by this publication may be available from other sources, which the user may wish to consult for additional views or information not covered by this publication.

PMI has no power, nor does it undertake to police or enforce compliance with the contents of this document. PMI does not certify, test, or inspect products, designs, or installations for safety or health purposes. Any certification or other statement of compliance with any health or safety-related information in this document shall not be attributable to PMI and is solely the responsibility of the certifier or maker of the statement.

TABLE OF CONTENTS

1

INTRODUCTION

This section defines several key terms and provides an overview of *The Standard for Portfolio Management –* Third Edition in the following major sections:

1.1 Purpose of *The Standard for Portfolio Management*

The increasing acceptance of portfolio management indicates that the application of appropriate knowledge, processes, skills, tools, and techniques to select the right work may have a significant impact on program, project, and organization success. *The Standard for Portfolio Management –* Third Edition identifies portfolio management processes generally recognized as good practices. "Generally recognized" means that the knowledge and practices described are applicable to most portfolios most of the time, and that there is widespread consensus about their value and usefulness. "Good practice" means there is general agreement that the application of these skills, tools, and techniques can enhance the chances of success over a wide range of portfolios. Good practice does not mean the knowledge described should always be applied uniformly to all portfolios; the organization and portfolio manager are responsible for determining what is appropriate for any given portfolio.

The Standard for Portfolio Management also provides and promotes a common vocabulary within the portfolio management profession for discussing, writing, and applying portfolio management concepts.

Portfolio management is intended for all types of organizations (e.g., profit, nonprofit, and government). When the term "organization" is used herein, it applies generally to these three types of organizations. A profit organization is an organization that exists primarily to yield a return for its owners. A nonprofit organization is an organization that does not distribute its surplus funds to owners or shareholders, but instead uses them to help pursue its goals. Government organizations exist under government ownership.

This standard is an expansion of and companion to information already provided in *A Guide to the Project Management Body of Knowledge (PMBOK® Guide)* – Fifth Edition [1],[1] *The Standard for Program Management* – Third Edition [2], and *Organizational Project Management Maturity Model (OPM3®)* – Third Edition [3]. As a foundational reference, this standard is neither intended to be comprehensive nor all-inclusive. This standard is a guide rather than a methodology. One can use different methodologies and tools to implement the processes described herein.

In addition to the standards that establish guidelines for project management processes, tools, and techniques, the *PMI® Code of Ethics and Professional Conduct* describes the expectations that practitioners should have of themselves and others. It is specific about the basic obligation of responsibility, respect, fairness, and honesty. It requires that practitioners demonstrate a commitment to ethical and professional conduct. It carries the obligation to comply with laws, regulations, and organizational and professional policies. Since practitioners come from diverse backgrounds and cultures, the *Code of Ethics and Professional Conduct* applies globally. When dealing with any stakeholder, practitioners should be committed to honest and fair practices and respectful dealings. The *PMI® Code of Ethics and Professional Conduct* is posted on the PMI® website (http://www.pmi.org). Acceptance and adherence to PMI's code of ethics is a requirement to achieve and maintain the PMP® and other PMI certification programs.

1.1.1 Audience for *The Standard for Portfolio Management*

This standard provides a foundational reference for anyone interested in managing a portfolio of projects, programs, and operations. This includes, but is not limited to:

- Senior executives who make decisions regarding organizational strategy;
- Management staff responsible for developing organizational strategy or those making recommendations to senior executives;
- Portfolio managers, program managers, and project managers;
- Researchers analyzing portfolio management;
- Managers of project and program managers;
- Members of a portfolio, program, or project management office;
- Consultants and other specialists in portfolio, program, or project management and related fields;
- Operations managers, organization unit managers, and process owners with financial, human, or material resources in a portfolio;
- Project team members, customers, and other stakeholders;
- Educators teaching the management of portfolios and related subjects; and
- Students of portfolio management.

---

[1] The numbers in brackets refer to the list of references at the end of this standard.

1.2 What is a Portfolio?

A portfolio is a component collection of programs, projects, or operations managed as a group to achieve strategic objectives. The portfolio components may not necessarily be interdependent or have related objectives. The portfolio components are quantifiable, that is, they can be measured, ranked, and prioritized.

A portfolio exists to achieve one or more organizational strategies and objectives and may consist of a set of past, current, and planned or future portfolio components. Portfolios and programs have the potential to be longer term with new projects rotating into the portfolios or programs, unlike projects that have a defined beginning and end.

An organization may have more than one portfolio, each addressing unique organizational strategies and objectives. Proposed initiatives are structured as portfolios and components are identified, evaluated, selected, and authorized. In addition, portfolios may contain subportfolios (see Figure 1-1).

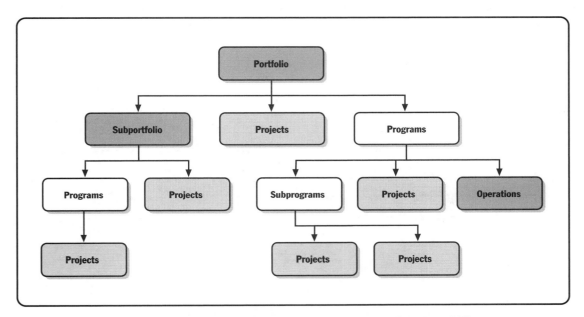

Figure 1-1. Portfolios, Programs, and Projects – High-Level View

At any given moment, a portfolio represents a view of its selected portfolio components and reflects the organizational strategy and objectives; even when specific projects or programs within the portfolio are not necessarily interdependent or have related objectives. By reflecting upon the investments made or planned by an organization, portfolio management includes the activities for identifying and aligning the organizational priorities; determining governance and performance management framework; measuring value/benefit; making investment decisions; and managing risk, communication, and resources.

If a portfolio is not aligned to its organizational strategy, the organization should reasonably question why the work is being undertaken. Therefore, a portfolio should be a representation of an organization's intent, direction, and progress.

1.2.1 Relationships Among Portfolios, Programs, and Projects

The relationship among portfolios, programs, and projects is such that a portfolio refers to a collection of projects, programs, subportfolios, and operations grouped together in order to facilitate the effective management of that work to meet strategic business objectives. Programs are grouped within a portfolio and are comprised of subprograms, projects, or operations that are managed in a coordinated fashion in support of the portfolio. Individual projects that are either within or outside of a program are still considered to be part of a portfolio. Although the projects or programs within the portfolio may not necessarily be interdependent or directly related, they are linked to the organization's strategic plan by means of the organization's portfolio.

As Figure 1-2 illustrates, organizational strategies and priorities are linked and have relationships between portfolios and programs, and between programs and individual projects. Organizational planning impacts the projects by means of project prioritization based on risk, funding, and other considerations relevant to the organization's strategic plan. Organizational planning can direct the management of resources and support for the component projects on the basis of risk categories, specific lines of business, or general types of projects, such as infrastructure and process improvement.

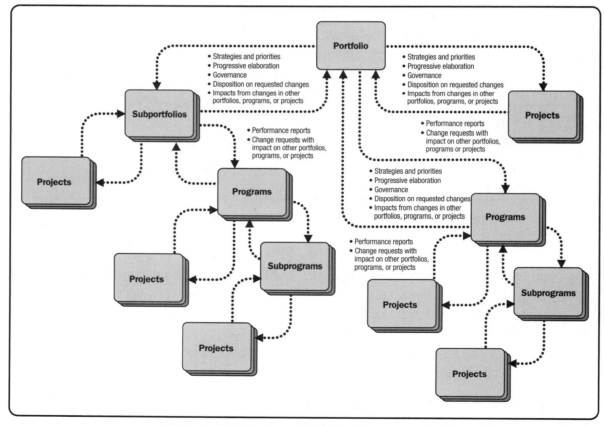

Figure 1-2. Portfolio, Program, and Project Management Interactions

All portfolio components of a portfolio should exhibit certain common features as follows:

- Be representative of investments made or planned by the organization;
- Be aligned with the organization's goals and objectives;
- Typically have some common features that permit the organization to group them for effective management;
- Have the ability to be quantifiable and, therefore, can be measured, ranked, and prioritized; and
- Share and compete for organizational resources.

Portfolio management ensures that interrelationships between programs and projects are identified and that resources (e.g., people, equipment, funding) are allocated in accordance with organizational priorities. Programs focus on achieving a specific set of benefits expected as determined by organizational strategy and objectives, while projects are largely concerned with creating specific deliverables that support specific organizational objectives and may or may not be part of program.

Portfolio management interacts with and impacts a number of organizational functions. Functional groups may be stakeholders in the portfolio and can also serve as sponsors of various portfolio components. The achievement of portfolio objectives may impact functional groups within an organization in their daily operations. Moreover, an operational budget may be influenced by portfolio management decisions, including allocation of resources to support portfolio components.

"Operations" is a term used to describe day-to-day organizational activities. The organization's operations may include, but are not limited to production, manufacturing, finance, marketing, legal, information services, human resources, and administrative services.

Processes and deliverables used by operations management are often outputs of the portfolio components. Therefore, the portfolio manager must manage relationships and interfaces with operations effectively if the full value of each portfolio component is to be realized.

1.3 What is Portfolio Management?

Portfolio management is the coordinated management of one or more portfolios to achieve organizational strategies and objectives. It includes interrelated organizational processes by which an organization evaluates, selects, prioritizes, and allocates its limited internal resources to best accomplish organizational strategies consistent with its vision, mission, and values. Portfolio management produces valuable information to support or alter organizational strategies and investment decisions.

Portfolio management provides an opportunity for a governing body to make decisions that control or influence the direction of a group of portfolio components as they work to achieve specific outcomes. An organization uses the processes, tools, and techniques described in this standard to identify, select, prioritize, govern, allocate resources, monitor, and report the contributions of the portfolio components to, and their relative alignment with, organizational objectives. *Portfolio management* balances conflicting demands between programs and projects, allocates resources (e.g., people, funding) based on organizational priorities and capacity, and manages so as to achieve the benefits identified. *Program management's* focus is on achieving the cost, schedule, and performance objectives of the projects within the program or portfolio. *Project management* is largely concerned with achieving specific deliverables that support specific organizational objectives.

The attributes of portfolio components can be further differentiated as represented in Table 1-1.

Table 1-1. Comparative Overview of Project, Program, and Portfolio Management

Organizational Project Management			
	PROJECTS	**PROGRAMS**	**PORTFOLIOS**
Scope	Projects have defined objectives. Scope is progressively elaborated throughout the project life cycle.	Programs have a larger scope and provide more significant benefits.	Portfolios have an organizational scope that changes with the strategic objectives of the organization.
Change	Project managers expect change and implement processes to keep change managed and controlled.	Program managers expect change from both inside and outside the program and are prepared to manage it.	Portfolio managers continuously monitor changes in the broader internal and external environment.
Planning	Project managers progressively elaborate high-level information into detailed plans throughout the project life cycle.	Program managers develop the overall program plan and create high-level plans to guide detailed planning at the component level.	Portfolio managers create and maintain necessary processes and communication relative to the aggregate portfolio.
Management	Project managers manage the project team to meet the project objectives.	Program managers manage the program staff and the project managers; they provide vision and overall leadership.	Portfolio managers may manage or coordinate portfolio management staff, or program and project staff that may have reporting responsibilities into the aggregate portfolio.
Success	Success is measured by product and project quality, timeliness, budget compliance, and degree of customer satisfaction.	Success is measured by the degree to which the program satisfies the needs and benefits for which it was undertaken.	Success is measured in terms of the aggregate investment performance and benefit realization of the portfolio.
Monitoring	Project managers monitor and control the work of producing the products, services, or results that the project was undertaken to produce.	Program managers monitor the progress of program components to ensure the overall goals, schedules, budget, and benefits of the program will be met.	Portfolio managers monitor strategic changes and aggregate resource allocation, performance results, and risk of the portfolio.

1.4 Relationships Between Portfolio Management, Program Management, Project Management, and Organizational Project Management

In order to understand portfolio, program, and project management, it is important to recognize the similarities and differences among these disciplines. It is also helpful to understand how they relate to organizational project management (OPM). OPM is a strategy execution framework utilizing project, program, and portfolio management as well as organizational-enabling practices to consistently and predictably deliver organizational strategy producing better performance, better results, and a sustainable competitive advantage.

Portfolio, program, and project management are required to be aligned with or be driven by organizational strategies. Conversely, portfolio, program, and project management differ in the way each contributes to the achievement of strategic goals. Portfolio management aligns with organizational strategies by selecting the right programs or projects, prioritizing the work and providing the needed resources. Program management harmonizes its project and program components, and manages their interdependencies in order to realize specified benefits. Project management develops and implements plans to achieve a specific scope that is driven by the objectives of the program or the portfolio to which it is subjected and, ultimately, to organizational strategies.

OPM advances organizational capability by linking project, program, and portfolio management principles and practices with organizational enablers (e.g. structural, cultural, technological, and human resource practices) to support strategic goals. An organization measures its capabilities, then plans and implements improvements towards the systematic achievement of best practices.

1.5 Portfolio Management and Organizational Strategy

Organizations are concerned that they possess an effective structure for management that will lead to the longevity and success of the organization. An organizational strategy is in part a plan of goals, policies, and actions that provide the overall direction and focus of the organization.

Portfolio management is an integral part of the organization's overall strategic plan. Organizational governance occurs at different decision-making levels of the organization to support specific goals, objectives, and strategies defined through the organization's strategic planning process. Organizational strategy and objectives define the means of attaining the goals through either operations (ongoing organizational activities) or programs and projects. In some organizations, operations and the management of programs and projects may fall under specific portfolios. Portfolio management is a bridge between organizational strategy, program, and project management and operations. As such, all governance levels are linked together to ensure that each organizational action is ultimately aligned with the defined organizational strategy.

Portfolio management ensures that an organization is able to leverage its project selection and execution success and support a strong and profitable organization within a competitive and rapidly changing organization environment. Portfolio management, program management, and project management are disciplines for managing the capability to deliver value. It is in operations management where delivery of value is realized through day-to-day processes. An organization establishes goals that will move it towards its vision. These goals will have objectives that are measures of goal achievement. Strategies are developed for how the goals will be achieved. These strategies direct the execution of work intended to achieve the goals. For the purposes of this standard, organizational strategy is a plan that describes how the organization's strengths and core competencies will be used to:

- Manage resources effectively;
- Manage stakeholder value;

- Capitalize on opportunities;
- Minimize the impact of threats;
- Respond to changes in the market, legal, and regulatory environments; and
- Reinforce focus on critical operational activities.

This standard presumes that the organization has an organizational strategy and objectives containing mission and vision statements as well as goals, objectives, and strategies intended to achieve the vision. Linking portfolio management to strategy balances the use of resources to maximize the value delivered in executing programs, projects, and operational activities.

The organizational strategy and objectives are translated into a set of initiatives that are influenced by many factors such as market dynamics, customer and partner requests, shareholders, government regulations, and competitor plans and actions. These initiatives establish portfolios of programs, projects, and operations components to be executed in the planned period.

Figure 1-3 depicts a general relationship between the programs, projects, and operational processes in an organization.

Figure 1-3. The Organizational Context of Portfolio Management

In Figure 1-3, vision, mission, and organizational strategy and objectives illustrate the relationship and the direction provided to portfolio management strategic planning and management of programs, projects, and operations. *Portfolio management*, through the alignment of the strategic planning establishes the portfolios required to achieve organizational strategy and objectives and performance goals. Management of authorized programs and projects *and* management of ongoing operations are required to execute portfolios consisting of programs, projects, and operations activities to realize the organizational strategy and objectives.

The shaded section in Figure 1-3, portfolio management strategic planning and management of programs, projects, and operations, depicts the relationship between organizational strategy and objectives and management activities. This relationship is highlighted due to the traditional focus of portfolio management on strategic program, project, and operations planning. To guide the management of authorized programs, projects, and operations, a portfolio is created. This portfolio, which links the organizational strategy to a set of prioritized programs, projects, and operations, addresses the relevant internal and external organization drivers referenced as objectives in the organizational strategy and objectives. Portfolio performance is monitored against the organizational strategy and objectives with performance feedback providing input to the potential change of strategic direction for the organization.

The ultimate goal of linking portfolio management with organizational strategy is to establish a balanced, executable plan that will help the organization achieve its goals. The impact of the portfolio plan upon strategy is attained by the six areas shown below:

- **Maintaining portfolio alignment.** Each portfolio component should be aligned to one or more strategic objectives. Alignment cannot occur without a clear understanding of those objectives, and any proposal for a portfolio component should describe how it supports the attainment of the objectives.

- **Allocating financial resources.** The priority of each portfolio component guides financial allocation decisions, while at the same time each portfolio component requires an allocation if it is to be executed.

- **Allocating human resources.** The priority of each portfolio component guides resource planning, hiring efforts, scheduling, and capability allocations, including long-range talent development.

- **Allocating material or equipment resources.** The priority of each portfolio component should be informational material, equipment, or space allocations, including long-range capital investments and planning that may be needed to ensure portfolio component needs are accounted for at an organizational level, including any constraints.

- **Measuring portfolio component performance.** If the purpose of undertaking the portfolio component is to achieve a strategic goal, its contribution must be measured in the context of that goal.

- **Managing risks.** Each portfolio component should be evaluated for risks (positive/opportunities, negative/threats, internal, external) at the organizational level and how those risks may impact the achievement of the strategic plan and objectives. This includes external as well as internal environment monitoring.

1.6 Business Value

Business value is a concept that is unique to each organization. Business value is defined as the entire value of the business—the total sum of all tangible and intangible elements. Examples of tangible elements include monetary assets, fixtures, stockholder equity, and utility. Examples of intangible elements include good will, brand recognition, public benefit, and trademarks. Depending on the organization, business value scope can be short-, medium-, or long-term. Value may be created through the effective management of ongoing operations. However, through the effective use of portfolio, program, and project management, organizations will possess the ability to employ reliable, established processes to meet strategic objectives and obtain greater business value from their project investments. While not all organizations are business driven, all organizations conduct activities. Whether an organization is a government agency or a nonprofit organization, all organizations focus on attaining value for their activities.

Successful business value realization begins with comprehensive strategic planning and management. Organizational strategy can be expressed through the organization's mission and vision, including orientation to markets, competition, and other environmental factors. Effective organizational strategy provides defined directions for development and growth, in addition to performance metrics for success. In order to bridge the gap between organizational strategy and successful business value realization, the use of portfolio, program, and project management techniques is essential.

Portfolio management aligns components (programs, projects, or operations) to the organizational strategy, organized into portfolios or subportfolios to optimize project or program objectives, dependencies, costs, timelines, benefits, resources, and risks. This allows organizations to have an overall view of how the strategic goals are reflected in the portfolio, institute appropriate governance management, and authorize human, financial, or material resources to be allocated based on expected performance and benefits.

Using program management, organizations have the ability to align multiple projects for optimized or integrated costs, schedule, effort, and benefits. Program management focuses on project interdependencies and helps to determine the optimal approach for managing and realizing the desired benefits.

With project management, organizations have the ability to apply knowledge, processes, skills, and tools and techniques that enhance the likelihood of success over a wide range of projects. Project management focuses on the successful delivery of products, services, or results. Within programs and portfolios, projects are a means of achieving organizational strategy and objectives.

Organizations can further facilitate the alignment of these portfolio, program, and project management activities by strengthening organizational enablers such as structural, cultural, technological, and human resource practices. By continuously conducting portfolio strategic alignment and optimization, performing business impact analyses, and developing robust organizational enablers, organizations can achieve successful transitions within the portfolio, program, and project domains and attain effective investment management and business value realization.

1.7 Portfolio Component Management Relationships

A portfolio has a parent-child relationship with its portfolio components, just as a program has a parent-child relationship with its projects. The portfolio components are managed according to frameworks, such as *A Guide to the*

Project Management Body of Knowledge (PMBOK® Guide) – Fifth Edition and *The Standard for Program Management* –Third Edition, and are periodically measured to gauge the likelihood of the portfolio components achieving their goals. An organization evaluates the portfolio components using the tools and techniques within the portfolio management processes, such as define, authorize, and optimize portfolio processes detailed later in this standard.

1.7.1 Program Management

Program management is the application of knowledge, skills, tools, and techniques to a program to meet the program requirements and to obtain benefits and control not available by managing the component projects individually. It involves aligning multiple components to achieve the program goals and allows for optimized or integrated cost, schedule, and effort.

Components within a program are related through a common outcome or delivery of a collective set of benefits. If the relationship among the projects is only that of a shared client, seller, technology, or resource, the effort should be managed as a portfolio of projects rather than as a program. In programs, it is important to integrate and control the interdependencies among the components. The program manager accomplishes this by working in five interrelated and interdependent Program Management Performance Domains: Program Strategy Alignment, Program Benefits Realization, Program Stakeholder Engagement, Program Governance, and Program Life Cycle Management. Through these Program Management Performance Domains, the program manager oversees component interdependencies and helps to determine the optimal approach for managing them. Actions related to these interdependencies may include:

- Coordinating common program activities, such as financing and procurement across all program components, work, or phases. Resolving resource constraints and conflicts that affect multiple components within the program;

- Responding effectively to risks spanning multiple components or across the entire program;

- Aligning program efforts with the organizational/strategic direction, which impacts and affects the portfolio;

- Resolving scope/cost/schedule/quality impacts within a shared governance structure; and

- Tailoring program management activities processes and interfaces to effectively address cultural, socio-economic, political, and environmental differences in globally oriented programs.

Through structured oversight and governance, program management enables appropriate planning, control, delivery, transition, and benefits sustainment across the components within the program to achieve the program's intended strategic benefits. Program management provides a framework for managing related efforts considering key factors such as strategic benefits, coordinated planning, complex interdependencies, deliverable integration, resource pools, and optimized pacing.

1.7.2 Project Management

Project management is the application of knowledge, skills, tools, and techniques to project activities to meet the project requirements. Project management is accomplished through the appropriate application and integration of project management processes comprising five Process Groups.

These five Process Groups are:

- Initiating,
- Planning,
- Executing,
- Monitoring and Controlling, and
- Closing.

Managing a project typically includes:

- Identifying requirements;
- Addressing the various needs, concerns, and expectations of the stakeholders, as the project is planned and carried out;
- Setting and maintaining active communication with stakeholders;
- Balancing the competing project constraints, which includes, but is not limited to:
  - Scope,
  - Quality,
  - Schedule,
  - Budget,
  - Resources, and
  - Risk.

The specific project circumstances may influence the constraints on which the project manager needs to focus.

The relationship among these factors is such that if any one factor changes, at least one other factor is likely to be affected. For example, if the schedule is shortened, often the budget needs to be increased to add additional resources to complete the same amount of work in less time. If a budget increase is not possible, the scope or quality may be reduced to deliver a product in less time for the same budget. Project stakeholders may have differing ideas as to which factors are the most important, creating an even greater challenge. Changing the project requirements may create additional risks. The project team should be able to assess the situation, balance the demands, and maintain active communication with stakeholders in order to deliver a successful project. It is important for the project team to be very conscious of how the success of the project fits into the organization's measures of success, which can be conveyed as part of the portfolio management process.

Because of the potential for change, the project management plan is iterative and goes through progressive elaboration throughout the project's life cycle. Progressive elaboration involves continuously improving and detailing a plan as more detailed and specific information and more accurate estimates become available. Progressive elaboration allows a project management team to manage to a greater level of detail as the project evolves.

1.7.3 Operations Management

Operations management constitutes all those activities of the organization that are ongoing and often cyclical in nature. Operations may be called the day-to-day activities. Operations management consists of the procedures and their assignment as roles with lines of delegation, levels of authority, and mechanisms to report, escalate, and decide how to achieve best value from resources available within constraints. When the ongoing pattern of activity is subject to change (by external factors for example) or when it may be improved by discretionary application of change, then resources within the portfolio are diverted into projects. Projects may be further grouped as programs (due to a link between their results or shared resources) and into portfolios due to a linkage between any or all of their schedule, resources, or stakeholders.

The portfolio of operational projects links a subset of recurring activities managed as projects to the organizational strategy. As operational projects and programs are delivered, the organization will have a solid foundation on which to execute strategic portfolio components.

The outputs from operations planning and organizational strategy and objectives result in portfolios that guide program and project activities. As the portfolio components move into initiation, the respective areas use their management processes to manage deliveries. As they are executed, portfolio management maintains the relationships between portfolio components to monitor progress and maintain alignment with strategic goals. Therefore, at the highest level, the strategic and operational portfolios are ultimately managed as a single, comprehensive portfolio of work being undertaken by the organization. The following organizational functions may be included in portfolio management:

- **Finance.** Effective management of the portfolio requires tangible, timely, and accurate financial information. The portfolio manager considers financial goals and objectives in the management of a portfolio. Therefore, the finance function may perform up-front project component proposal evaluation, monitor portfolio budgets, compare project spending with the allocated budget, and examine benefits realized. This ensures that financial plan adjustments are made and the projected financial benefits are quantifiable and delivered.

- **Marketing.** Market analysis, benchmarking, and research play a significant role in portfolio management as the portfolio components are driven by such considerations as market opportunity or competitive advantage. For a nonprofit or government organization, a similar analysis of value-for-money or value-to-organizational-mission is needed for portfolio component selection and management.

- **Human resources.** By looking at the portfolio components, the human resources function can identify the skills, qualifications, and other requisites needed for success, then work to ensure skilled resources are available when needed. The human resources function also works to facilitate resource realignment and mitigate the negative impact on people and organizational elements resulting from organizational changes that occur when portfolio components are delivered.

- **Information technology.** Portfolio management usually has a significant impact on information technology operations. Portfolio components often require support from information technology operations, including organization process analysis, development, service, help desk support, infrastructure support, and ongoing application maintenance. For example, a manufacturing portfolio contains a program to install an enterprise resource planning (ERP) system for the organization. This portfolio could potentially increase help desk support, network traffic, and support obligations for an application development team. The portfolio manager needs to take these factors into account to ensure that infrastructure and properly trained resources are adequate to support the portfolio's components.

- **Quality management.** Quality management ensures conformance with voluntary standards, such as ISO standards for quality management, that the organization has chosen to follow as part of a business practice or a contractual obligation. Additionally, either within the quality management mandate or as a separate responsibility, the organization has responsibilities for regulatory compliance management. The portfolio manager has a fiduciary duty to follow the organization's commitments to conformance with applicable voluntary standards and compliance with regulatory requirements.

1.8 Role of the Portfolio Manager

Portfolio managers are responsible for the execution of the portfolio management process. Where program and project managers focus on "doing work right," portfolio managers focus on "doing the right work." Portfolio managers receive information on portfolio component performance and progress, and they convey to the portfolio management governing body how the portfolio components as a whole are aligned with the strategic goals, then provide appropriate recommendations or options for action. They also ensure that timetables for portfolio management processes are maintained and followed and that the managers of portfolio components (projects, programs, and operations) receive and provide the information required under the portfolio management processes. They are the primary conduit between managers of portfolio components and portfolio stakeholders.

The portfolio manager may be an individual, a group, or a governing body, and is responsible for establishing, monitoring, and managing all assigned portfolios. Specific responsibilities may include:

- Establishing and maintaining a framework (a conceptual and communicable structure of ideas) and methodology (a body of policies and procedures) for portfolio management within the organization;

- Establishing and maintaining relevant portfolio management processes (strategic management, governance management, communication management, performance management, and risk management);

- Guiding the selection, prioritization, balancing, and termination of portfolio components to ensure the alignment with strategic goals and organizational priorities;

- Establishing and maintaining appropriate infrastructure and systems to support portfolio management processes;

- Continuously reviewing, reallocating, reprioritizing, and optimizing the portfolio to ensure ongoing alignment with evolving organizational goals and market opportunities and threats;

- Providing key stakeholders with timely assessment of portfolio component selection, prioritization, and performance, as well as early identification of (and intervention in) portfolio-level issues and risks that are impacting performance;

- Measuring and monitoring the value to the organization through portfolio performance metrics and targets, such as benefit ratios, return on investment (ROI), net present value (NPV), payback period (PP), internal rate of return (IRR), and scorecards. Government and not-for-profit organizations may have other measures and targets;

- Meeting legal and regulatory requirements;

- Achieving the information needs of current or future stakeholders;

- Supporting senior-level decision making by ensuring timely and consistent communication to stakeholders on progress, changes, and impact on portfolio components;

- Influencing active executive sponsorship engagement for the portfolio and each portfolio component as it is initiated; and

- Participating in program and project reviews to reflect senior-level support, leadership, and involvement in key decisions.

1.8.1 Knowledge and Skills

The portfolio manager needs to be aware of how the portfolio is related to the organizational strategy and assess and measure the benefits that the portfolio is adding to the organization's objectives. Throughout the portfolio life cycle, the portfolio manager should be able to manage risks, monitor and prioritize portfolio components, resolve issues that need senior-level attention, develop and improve processes, and apply organization knowledge and management skills. In addition, the portfolio manager should be able to effectively manage the organization's resources and provide timely information for stakeholder communication requirements.

In order to succeed in this role, the portfolio manager should have expertise in all of the following areas.

- **Portfolio strategic management and alignment.** A portfolio manager should understand and monitor changes in the organizational strategy and objectives and be aware of how the portfolio supports them. Both financial and nonfinancial benefits and risks to the organization need to be taken into account. The portfolio manager typically does not create organizational strategy and objectives, but may participate in the process depending on the specific organization. However, the portfolio manager does play a key role in creating the portfolio strategic plan and implementing the strategy by monitoring the execution of initiatives in support of the plan and by communicating progress and results.

- **Portfolio management methods and techniques.** The portfolio manager should have expertise in the application and analysis of portfolio management methods and techniques that include both qualitative and quantitative measures. Some examples are:

  o Decision support tools and models, simulation techniques, and constraint management;

  o Prioritization algorithms;

- ○ Capability and capacity modeling methods and tools;

- ○ Project and program auditing techniques;

- ○ Organizational management;

- ○ Portfolio risk management;

- ○ Program and project management methods and techniques;

- ○ Organizational, industry, and domain acumen, which cover relevant markets, the customer base, competition, trends, standards, legal and regulatory environments, and appropriate code of conduct;

- ○ Financial analysis and management concepts, such as risk, return, financial capital, budgeting, and variance reporting;

- ○ Portfolio performance metrics and targets;

- ○ Portfolio component proposal preparation, evaluation, and selection techniques; and

- ○ Resource management and productivity improvement methods and techniques.

- **Stakeholder engagement.** An effective portfolio manager is adept at working with portfolio stakeholders in order to maximize portfolio and organizational performance. A portfolio manager should communicate frequently with stakeholders using modes and techniques appropriate for the context. The portfolio manager should facilitate communications between stakeholders to negotiate agreements and make portfolio decisions.

- **Leadership and management skills.** An effective portfolio manager has well-developed leadership and management skills and is able to interact with executives, management, and other stakeholders. Further, a portfolio manager is adept in managing people through recruitment and retention, goal-setting, performance evaluation, reward and recognition, succession planning, and employee development. Employee development may include mentoring, coaching, motivating, and training of personnel.

General management skills should be exercised in alignment with the organization's culture, maturity, and policies and also with regard to cultural and other differences between individuals. In addition, the portfolio manager should possess and display well-developed skills in communication, team building, planning, conflict management, negotiation, meeting facilitation, decision making, and dealing with organizational barriers to success. The portfolio manager needs to be able to adapt to a wide range of organizational decision-making models, from autocratic to academic.

- **Risk management.** An effective portfolio manager manages risks that are internal and external to the organization as well as threats and opportunities. For risk evaluation, consideration is given to portfolio dynamics, such as fiscal constraints, cost-benefit, windows of opportunity, portfolio component constraints, and stakeholder dynamics. Risk management is a structured process for assessing and analyzing portfolio risks [threats and opportunities] with the goal of capitalizing on the potential opportunities and mitigating (one of several risk responses) those events, activities, or circumstances that can adversely impact the portfolio. Risk threat management is critical where interdependencies exist between high-priority portfolio components, where the cost of portfolio component failure is significant, or when risks of one portfolio component increase the risks in another portfolio component. Opportunity management identifies and exploits or enhances the potential improvements in portfolio component performance that may increase quality, customer satisfaction, service levels, and productivity for both the portfolio components and the organization. Opportunity management may generate new portfolio components.

1.9. Role of the PMO in Portfolio Management

PMO refers to a project, program, or portfolio management office and supports project, program, or portfolio functions respectively. The PMO in an organization is the entity that defines and maintains the process standards generally related to project, program, or portfolio management. At a basic level, the PMO may handle communication in the form of status reporting.

The PMO is generally assigned various responsibilities related to the projects, programs, and portfolios that fall within its assigned functions. It provides guidance on the practice of portfolio or program or project management within the organization; however, in some organizations, the PMO may be involved in project execution, such as facilitation, process management, and supporting implementation of project management methodologies.

Depending on the organizational structure, the PMO either functions on an enterprise-wide level, or as one of many departmental PMOs that manage projects from different departments or divisions within an organization. There may also be special purpose PMOs based on the needs of the organization. The specific form, function, and structure of a PMO are dependent upon the needs of the organization and the stakeholders.

A PMO may support portfolio management in the following ways:

- Managing portfolio components, supporting component proposals and evaluations, facilitating prioritization and authorization, and allocating resources in alignment with organizational strategy and objectives;
- Developing and maintaining portfolio, program, and project frameworks and methodologies;
- Providing project and program progress information and metric reporting (e.g., expenditure, defects, resources) to the portfolio governance process;
- Negotiating and coordinating resources between various portfolio components or between portfolios;
- Assisting with risk identification and risk strategy development and communicating risks and issues related to portfolio components;
- Coordinating communication across portfolio components;
- Developing and improving templates and checklists;
- Monitoring compliance to policies;
- Providing knowledge management including lessons learned; and

- Developing and conducting training and mentoring human resources in portfolio management skills, tools, and techniques.

1.9.1 Project, Program, or Portfolio Management Office

The structure and responsibilities of a project, program, or portfolio management office depends upon the needs of the organization. The PMO coordinates the management of its assigned portfolio components. The assigned responsibility may be a specific area of the organization or a class of projects or programs. The responsibilities of a management office can include the following:

- Provide project or program management support functions,
- Manage day-to-day operations of the system or systems that support portfolio management, and
- Resource and directly manage a portfolio component or category of portfolio components.

The role, responsibilities, and activities of a management office are addressed in the relevant PMI standards: *A Guide to the Project Management Body of Knowledge (PMBOK® Guide)* – Fifth Edition and *The Standard for Program Management* – Third Edition.

The establishment of a PMO may highlight the need for a structured and formal governance process and body in the case where none existed previously. This, in turn, generates further benefits, discipline, and understanding for the organization. This newly established, revitalized, or realigned governing body is responsible for establishing the expectations for the derived benefits of portfolio management as the implementation of portfolio management processes is authorized.

The portfolio management office has a focused and specific responsibility for the centralized management and coordination of the portfolios that lie in its domain. The responsibilities of this office may range from providing portfolio support functions to actually managing the portfolio. The structure and function of the portfolio management office may vary with the needs of the organization.

The portfolio management office may act as a stakeholder throughout the portfolio life cycle and may recommend the selection, termination, or initiation of actions necessary to ensure that the portfolio remains aligned with the organization strategic objectives.

The portfolio management office may provide the following services to a project or program management office:

- Aggregate and provide performance results of the portfolio components;
- Define portfolio management methodology, best practices, and standards for use as guidelines while formulating the methodology and standards for project and program management;
- Forecast supply and demand for a portfolio that can be further broken down into supply and demand for projects and programs;
- Define a portfolio management strategy;
- Provide portfolio oversight and manage the overall portfolio value; and
- Identify risks, analyze risks, and plan risk responses at a portfolio level.

1.9.2 Project Team

A project team plans and executes activities on a project to ensure the project achieves its objectives. The team also provides project performance metrics and progress as inputs to the portfolio management process.

1.9.3 Program Managers

The program manager is responsible for ensuring that the overall program structure and program management processes align with the portfolio management plan and enable the project teams to successfully complete their work. The program manager ensures that project deliverables are able to be integrated into the program's end product, service, results, and benefits. Program managers also ensure that the projects are organized and executed in a consistent manner and fulfilled within established standards.

The PMO supports the program manager by providing the information needed to make decisions that guide the program and by providing administrative support in managing schedules, budgets, risks, and other areas required for effective program management. A program manager works with the portfolio management team and/or office to provide information such as program and project performance against goals.

1.9.4 Project Managers

Project managers are responsible for the effective planning, execution, monitoring, and delivery of assigned projects in accordance with corresponding objectives and specifications. Project managers provide project performance indicators, directly or indirectly, to the portfolio manager, PMO, or governing body. This information is used with other criteria to determine which projects should proceed, be modified, suspended, or terminated and to communicate with stakeholders.

1.9.5 Portfolio Governance

Portfolio governance is established by a governing body to make decisions about investments and priorities for the portfolio and ensures the portfolio management processes are followed to sustain the organization. The governing body is made up of one or more individuals with the requisite authority, knowledge, and experience to ensure the alignment of portfolio components with organizational strategy. The governing body has the authority to evaluate the portfolio performance and to make resourcing, investment, and priority decisions as needed. Recommendations may include new portfolio components, the suspension or change of existing portfolio components, and the reallocation of resources among portfolio components. The recommendations may be complex with significant organizational constraints especially concerning reallocation of resources.

1.9.6 Sponsors

A sponsor is a person or group who provides resources and support for the project, program, or portfolio, and is accountable for enabling success. Sponsors champion the approval of portfolio components (projects, programs, and operations). To ensure approval, a sponsor assists by supplying a viable component proposal to the portfolio management governing body, other oversight group, or individual. Once the portfolio component is approved, the sponsor helps ensure that the components perform according to organizational strategy and objectives. Sponsors also recommend portfolio component changes or closures to align with organizational strategic changes.

1.10 Portfolio Management Body of Knowledge

This standard describes the summary of knowledge within the profession of portfolio management. The complete portfolio management body of knowledge includes proven traditional practices that are widely applied and innovative practices that are emerging in the profession. The portfolio management body of knowledge is constantly evolving. This standard represents generally recognized good practices for managing portfolios in any type of organization. These practices are applicable to most portfolios most of the time. In addition, this standard also defines the portfolio management processes, tools, and techniques used to manage a portfolio so that it remains aligned with the organizational strategy and objectives.

This standard focuses on processes that are unique to the portfolio management field, which is a subset of the portfolio management body of knowledge, and has interrelationships to its allied disciplines such as program and project management. Other standards may be consulted for additional information. *The Standard for Program Management* – Third Edition describes the guidelines for management of programs, and the *PMBOK® Guide* – Fifth Edition describes the management of projects. Examination of an organization's project management process maturity and capabilities is addressed in *OPM3®* – Third Edition. As a foundational reference, this standard is neither intended to be comprehensive nor all-inclusive.

2

PORTFOLIO MANAGEMENT OVERVIEW AND ORGANIZATION

This section describes the portfolio management context in the following sections:

2.1 Portfolio Management and Organizational Strategy and Objectives

2.2 Portfolio Management Process Implementation

2.3 Portfolio Management Process Cycle

2.4 Portfolio Management Information System (PMIS)

2.5 Portfolio Management Governance

2.6 Portfolio Stakeholders

2.7 Organizational influences on Portfolio Management

2.1 Portfolio Management and Organizational Strategy and Objectives

Portfolio management is a discipline that enables executive management to meet organizational strategy and objectives through efficient decision making concerning projects, programs, and operations. Portfolio management is performed in an environment broader than the portfolio itself. Portfolio management roles and processes span the organization.

Portfolio management includes processes to identify, categorize, monitor, evaluate, select, prioritize, balance, and authorize portfolio components within the portfolio. The portfolio managers may evaluate the performance of portfolio components and the portfolio as a whole in relation to the key indicators and the organizational strategy and objectives. During a typical organization cycle, the portfolio manager monitors, evaluates, and validates portfolio components relative to the following:

- Alignment with organizational strategy and objectives,
- Viability as part of the portfolio, based on key performance indicators and an acceptable level of risk,
- Value/benefit and relationship to other portfolio components,
- Available resources and portfolio priorities, and
- Additions and deletions of portfolio components.

The executive level, through the definition and articulation of the organizational strategy and objectives, determines the overall organizational strategy. The organizational strategy and objectives are inputs to the portfolio management process. These inputs drive the portfolio management process to ensure that portfolio components are aligned to achieve the organization's goals. Based on these inputs, the portfolio manager will use an accepted process to select, prioritize, and approve proposed portfolio components to begin. The portfolio manager should establish criteria for governance actions, such as deciding when projects/programs should proceed, be terminated, or suspended prior to originally planned completion dates. Through the review of strategic, tactical, and operational capabilities and gaps, the portfolio management process provides feedback that is useful for the planning and management of resource demand and for monitoring the health of the portfolio. The portfolio manager should report portfolio performance as it relates to achieving the organizational strategy.

The portfolio manager should also review the portfolio for balance (short-term versus long-term risk versus return) and negotiate agreement(s) with relevant strategic stakeholders (e.g., executive management, operations, or program management).

The portfolio manager should also sequence the portfolio components in the portfolio to account for portfolio component interdependencies, balancing of constrained resources, and other organizational considerations.

Once a portfolio component is authorized, the program/project manager assumes direct management control of the portfolio component and applies the appropriate management processes in an effort to ensure that the work is done effectively and efficiently. The responsible program/project managers will monitor planned to actual performance (schedule, budget, resources, quality, and scope) and will provide feedback to the portfolio manager. The processes for project and program management are described in these PMI standards: The *PMBOK® Guide –* Fifth Edition and *The Standard for Program Management –* Third Edition.

The portfolio management process also requires integration with the organizational strategy planning process to analyze current business opportunities or threats and to define strategic objectives. This drives strategic changes to ensure that the planned (active and future) portfolio components continue to support the strategic goals. For example, if the organizational strategic planning process determines that a goal is no longer valid for the organization, the portfolio manager should review the portfolio and recommend the reassessment of any portfolio components that are in place to achieve the obsolete goal. Organizations normally apply some form of control over portfolio components. For example, a phase-gate review is commonly applied to projects in those portfolios concentrating on research activities. Governance processes are often characterized by regular reviews at key decision milestones during the life of the project. Senior stakeholders in governance roles analyze the risk and benefits associated with continuing the project. The purpose of this analysis should be to assess the probability of success for various aspects of the project component at multiple milestone points during the life cycle of that component. Such "gate analysis" should be conducted at the portfolio review meetings. For instance, the legal, engineering, financial, and commercial aspects of the product are included in the early-stage assessments when the immediate investment decision is about research and development. As the project progresses, the legal, engineering, scientific, and other aspects continue to be assessed. Assessment results support governance decision making and are stored as portfolio information.

2.2 Portfolio Management Process Implementation

Portfolio management processes are typically started in organizations at a department or business unit level as a response to issues, conflicts, constrained resources, and uncertainty in the group, often around what work is being done and should be done. A structured approach to implement portfolio management processes may add long-term value to the business unit or at the organization level.

The steps for implementing a portfolio management process are those used to implement any process in an organization. They are:

- Assess the current state of the portfolio management process,
- Define the portfolio management vision and plan,
- Implement the portfolio management processes, and
- Improve the portfolio management processes.

2.2.1 Assess the Current State of the Portfolio Management Process

Performing an assessment of the current state of portfolio management and related processes provides insight as to what processes already exist, which processes are needed in the organization, and possible organizational or cultural enablers or barriers that will be encountered. An assessment will facilitate development of a gap analysis and plan to establish or formalize the portfolio management function.

Assessment activities may include:

- Identify and evaluate existing portfolio management knowledge (i.e., strategic management, governance, communications, risk management, and performance management);
- Assess the existing portfolio management processes to determine if they support organizational vision, mission, strategy, and objectives (i.e., processes that define, align, and authorize portfolio components);
- Assess the current portfolio management structure and resources for maturity and adequacy;
- Identify gaps in knowledge, processes, structure, and resources;
- Evaluate the existing portfolio components to determine if they are supportive of current organizational strategy and objectives;
- Assess the current portfolio component resource availability and allocations against the integrated schedule;
- Understand the stakeholders for each of the strategic objectives and portfolio components; and
- Review the existing portfolio reporting processes and procedures.

Assessment results may include:

- Depth and breadth of board of directors, executives, and senior management commitment;
- Level of satisfaction with the current practices;
- Communication goals and requirements of the organization;
- Misinformation that needs to be addressed;
- Project, program, portfolio, and operations management practices in place; and

- Understanding of the organization's vision, both long-term and short-term, for portfolio management.

OPM3® is one example of a tool that can be used for portfolio management assessment within an organization. The maturity assessments permit organizations to identify which best practices, capabilities, and outcomes they currently exhibit. The flexibility of the maturity assessment process permits an organization to focus on specific functions (project, program, and portfolio). These assessments allow the organization to identify gaps in best practices, capabilities, or outcomes it currently utilizes.

2.2.2   Define the Portfolio Management Vision and Plan

The portfolio management vision should be in alignment with the organizational vision and be supportive of the strategy and objectives of the organization. The vision for portfolio management will help to clarify the direction in which to proceed. The vision for portfolio management should reflect the organization's cultural values and should be meaningful and valid to stakeholders.

The organizational vision, strategy, and objectives will guide the interim steps needed to implement the portfolio management vision. A portfolio management roadmap is built for the implementation of organizational level portfolio management structure and processes. The organizational portfolio management implementation plan should address two related efforts in order to successfully establish a portfolio management process. They are:

- A planned approach to change organizational behavior that includes a balance of strong leadership and management, and a proficient management team commitment to the effort; and
- A planned approach for incrementally developing and implementing portfolio management processes, building on processes that already exist, and working towards the defined vision.

2.2.3   Implement the Portfolio Management Processes

Portfolio management processes are performed in an environment broader than a portfolio; therefore, an organization-level implementation team supported by executive management, a governing body, and portfolio managers may use this portfolio management standard as a guide to implement organization-level portfolio management processes. Key first steps will include:

- Define roles and responsibilities for portfolio management process implementation,
- Communicate the portfolio management implementation plan, and
- Define and deploy detailed portfolio management processes and provide training to staff and stakeholders.

Changing business processes within an organization may be a difficult undertaking. Planning for organizational and behavioral changes is required for a long-term successful implementation of the portfolio management processes. Much has been written on approaches to driving organizational change, however, this is beyond the scope of this standard.

2.2.4   Improve the Portfolio Management Processes

A portfolio management process improvement plan defines the objectives expected to be achieved from portfolio management and guides, measures, and prioritizes improvement activity. In addition, predefined metrics drive results and accountability for performance improvement. Metrics provide insight into the current performance of the processes as well as the results from changes to these processes. A documented process improvement plan may be advantageous to evaluate and improve current portfolio management processes. To ensure that the changes are implemented in a controlled manner, it is important to specify and manage changes to the processes, procedures, and tools used for portfolio management. Once the changes have been implemented, they should be monitored in order to validate the achievement of expected results.

In addition to the portfolio management processes, it is important to identify any dependent or parallel processes that will impact portfolio management performance. For example, the project management processes will impact the portfolio management process if the project process does not provide transparency to the performance of the project impacting the portfolio management selection process.

2.3 Portfolio Management Process Cycle

Organizations have many standard and recurring processes, including portfolio management. External requirements (such as fiscal reporting) or internal requirements (such as quarterly budget revisions) may drive these organizational processes as well as portfolio management processes. While portfolio management is a continuous process (unlike project or program management, which have a scheduled start and end), certain activities may follow a recurring timeframe, such as annually or as determined by the organization. The purpose is to integrate portfolio management process activities in those other organization processes. For example, selection and authorization of portfolio components can be part of the annual planning or strategic review with quarterly, monthly, and/or weekly updates. Performance monitoring of the portfolio is usually continuous. Revising the portfolio mix may be required when disruptions to the organization occur. Once established, the portfolio management process is continuous.

2.4 Portfolio Management Information System (PMIS)

The portfolio management information system (PMIS) consists of the tools and techniques used to gather, integrate, and disseminate the outputs of the portfolio management processes. It is used to support aspects of the portfolio processes and may include both manual and automated systems.

These systems support overall organizational visibility, standardization, measurement, and process improvement, and can facilitate effective decision making by providing the organization with key performance metrics and target collection, analysis, and reporting.

Automated tools may include commercial project portfolio management (PPM) applications, an information collection and distribution system, and web interfaces to other online automated systems to consolidate the portfolio components' status. The portfolio management information system is often a collection of spreadsheets rather than automated tools. An effective PMIS enables the portfolio manager to define, analyze, design, produce, and manage information systems to support a successful portfolio, and includes tools and processes such as:

- Software tools,
- Document repository and document version control systems,
- Change or configuration management systems,
- Risk database and analysis tools,
- Financial management processes and systems,
- Earned value management processes and tools,
- Communication management processes and tools, and
- Other knowledge management tools and processes required to support portfolio management.

2.5 Portfolio Management Governance

A cross-functional and integrated governing body determines and authorizes the scope of portfolio management governance to direct portfolio management oversight and operational activity. Input to the portfolio alignment decision-making process includes, but is not limited to, the organization vision, implementation strategy, resource capacity, and short- and long-term organization plans. In smaller organizations, executive management may assume all or some of the portfolio management governance responsibilities including making portfolio oversight decisions.

2.6 Portfolio Stakeholders

Portfolio stakeholders are individuals or groups whose interests may be positively or negatively affected by portfolio components or portfolio management processes. They may also exert influence over the portfolio, its portfolio components, processes, and decisions. The level of involvement by stakeholders may vary from organization to organization or from portfolio to portfolio within an organization.

Depending upon the size and type of the organization as well as project and program management practices, certain stakeholders may be specifically identified according to the goals and risk management strategies for the portfolio.

Stakeholders may include but are not limited to CEO and other executives, functional management, operations management, legal, finance, human resources, PMO, and program/project teams.

2.7 Organizational Influences on Portfolio Management

Successful portfolio management requires all management levels to support and communicate the value of portfolio management to the organization and external stakeholders.

When making portfolio decisions, organizations are influenced by a variety of constraints and dynamics brought by the stakeholders. Portfolio management is to balance stakeholder interests, both short-term and long-term, while staying aligned with the organizational strategy and objectives and considering resource constraints. The portfolio manager needs to make decisions in the best interest of the organizational strategy and objectives regardless of the impact to individual portfolio components, including portfolio component termination. Examples of forces influencing portfolio management are specified in the following sections.

2.7.1 Organizational Maturity

The organization as a whole should understand the organization's need for portfolio management and commit its leadership, resources (i.e., people, capital, and equipment), processes, and tools to make it successful. It is important that the philosophy of portfolio management permeates the entire organization. This means that all other activities and processes take into account the impact on or influence of portfolio management, even if the effect is slight. For instance, general performance measures should be compatible and complementary with those used for assessing portfolio components.

The term organizational maturity may be applied to the acceptance of portfolio management in the same way as it may apply to project management. The level of application and the success of portfolio management are directly affected by the level of maturity in the organization. Lack of organizational support for the concept and approach of portfolio management is a major obstacle to portfolio management success. The portfolio management process and the decisions resulting from it should be accepted by all levels within the organization. There is a risk or threat that, while the process is accepted by senior executives in the organization, the resulting decisions may not be accepted. Acceptance of portfolio management processes and decisions throughout the organization are necessary for portfolio management success. Another important element is the organization's ability to implement the changes recommended by the portfolio management processes. The ability to execute change is different from lack of acceptance of the recommendations and refers to an inability to make the desired changes. Not recognizing and formalizing the organization's ability to handle change is also a major obstacle to fully realizing the benefits expected from the portfolio. Each portfolio component should consistently apply similar techniques to facilitate and handle organizational change. The extent of organizational change that the organization is able to accept may be one of the factors used to determine the appropriate mix of portfolio components. This is related to the strategic objectives of the organization which serve as inputs to the portfolio decision process. Strategic goals will precipitate some expected level of change to the organization's people, processes, products, and technologies.

2.7.2 Organizational Impacts

This topic is related to that of organizational maturity described in Section 2.7.1. The distinction is that organizational impact refers to the impact that portfolio management has on the organization rather than on the organizational maturity in which portfolio management operates.

Effective portfolio management may have positive impacts across the organization by facilitating tactical and operational planning in alignment with strategic goals. Conversely, the lack of efficient and effective processes and procedures in other functional areas of the organization may also have a considerable impact on portfolio management. An example is the lack of an effective resource assignment process to support the execution of projects and programs approved through the portfolio management processes. Those involved in the portfolio management process will need to factor organizational impacts into the corresponding plans and decisions.

3

PORTFOLIO MANAGEMENT PROCESS GROUPS

Portfolio management is the centralized management of one or more portfolios that enables executive management to meet organizational goals and objectives through efficient decision making concerning one or more portfolios, projects, programs, and operations. Portfolio management is performed in an environment broader than the portfolio itself. Its roles and processes span the organization. The portfolio components, framework, and management processes are selected to produce specific benefits to the organization; therefore, selecting and tailoring portfolio management processes is a strategic decision.

In order to be successful, the portfolio manager's activities include, but are not limited to:

- Understanding the organizational strategy;
- Establishing strategic organizational criteria for managing the portfolio;
- Considering all of the organization's projects, programs, and other portfolio components; and
- Following agreed-upon processes mandated by the organization or selected by the team.

Portfolio management, as a set of strategic organizational processes, is a multitiered system consisting of strategic, functional, and operational organizational portfolio components. Portfolio management is planned and executed at all three tiers in the organization.

In addition to the organizational portfolio components, there are cross-functional teams involved, including executive management, the portfolio management office, functional and operations management, and the program and project management teams. The organizational portfolio components and cross-functional teams all add to the complexity of portfolio management processes.

Portfolio management is accomplished through processes using relevant knowledge, skills, tools, and techniques that receive inputs and generate outputs. A process within the context of portfolio management is a set of interrelated actions and activities performed to achieve a strategic element such as a goal, objective, or action to result in a benefit to the organization within the terms of strategic planning. Each process is characterized by its inputs, tools and techniques that may be applied, and the resulting outputs. A portfolio manager needs to understand the impact of the selected portfolio management processes on the expected organization results, which are delivered by the portfolio.

This standard covers the processes required to make decisions about portfolio components and identifies those portfolio management processes that have been recognized as generally accepted practices for project portfolios. These processes apply globally and across industry groups. Generally accepted practice means there is general agreement that the application of these portfolio management processes enhances the probability of success over time.

This does not mean that the processes described should always be applied uniformly for all portfolios. Each portfolio manager is responsible for tailoring the processes to be used; in other words, determining which processes are appropriate for a given portfolio.

Portfolio managers carefully address each process and its constituent inputs and outputs. They should use this standard as a high-level guide for those processes that are considered when managing a portfolio, including selecting and tailoring processes to ensure the right organizational and portfolio fit.

Portfolio management is an integrated undertaking requiring organizational strategy, the program, project and other management processes, including the portfolio management processes to be aligned and connected. Portfolios exist within an organization and should not operate as a closed system. Portfolios require input data from the organization and others, and deliver capabilities and other benefits back to the organization. Actions taken during one process typically affect that process and related processes. For example, an organizational strategic change may affect the portfolio roadmap, but it may also affect the portfolio communication and risk management plans. These process interactions often require tradeoffs among portfolio, program, and project requirements and objectives, which will vary from portfolio to portfolio and organization to organization. Successful portfolio management includes actively managing these interactions to meet executive management, sponsor, customer, and other stakeholder needs. In some circumstances, a process or set of processes will need to be iterated several times in order to achieve the desired outcome.

This standard describes the key elements of portfolio management. This standard is not prescriptive in nature and therefore does not specify the means by which an organization should implement the portfolio management processes described herein. This standard presumes that the organization has an organizational strategy and objectives accompanied by vision and mission statements as well as strategic goals and objectives. In order to implement the portfolio processes presented here, the following organizational enablers are needed:

- The organization—including executive management—embraces the practice of portfolio management;
- Proposed projects, programs and operational components need to be evaluated;
- Appropriately skilled staff members are available to manage the portfolio;
- Project and program management processes exist;
- The organizational roles and responsibilities are defined; and
- Mechanisms are in place to communicate decisions and other information internally and externally to the organization.

The remainder of this section provides information and interlinks processes for establishing and managing portfolio components, details the Process Groups, and includes the following major sections:

3.1 Portfolio Management Process Groups

3.1.1 Defining Process Group

3.1.2 Aligning Process Group

3.1.3 Authorizing and Controlling Process Group

3.2 Portfolio Management Process Interactions

3.1 Portfolio Management Process Groups

The following sections identify and describe the Portfolio Management Process Groups. These Process Groups have clear dependencies and are typically performed in the same sequence for each portfolio. They are independent of application areas or industry focus. The portfolio manager may repeat individual Process Groups and individual constituent processes prior to portfolio component authorization.

A Process Group includes the constituent portfolio management processes that are linked by the respective inputs and outputs, where the result or outcome of one process becomes the input to another. The Process Groups should not be thought of as portfolio management phases. Table 3-1 reflects the mapping of the 16 portfolio management processes into the three Portfolio Management Process Groups and the five Portfolio Management Knowledge Areas. Each of the key portfolio management processes is shown in the Process Group in which most of the activity takes place.

Table 3-1. Portfolio Management Process Groups and Knowledge Areas Mapping

Knowledge Areas	Process Groups		
	Defining Process Group	Aligning Process Group	Authorizing and Controlling Process Group
Portfolio Strategic Management	4.1 Develop Portfolio Strategic Plan 4.2 Develop Portfolio Charter 4.3 Define Portfolio Roadmap	4.4 Manage Strategic Change	
Portfolio Governance Management	5.1 Develop Portfolio Management Plan 5.2 Define Portfolio	5.3 Optimize Portfolio	5.4 Authorize Portfolio 5.5 Provide Portfolio Oversight
Portfolio Performance Management	6.1 Develop Portfolio Performance Management Plan	6.2 Manage Supply and Demand 6.3 Manage Portfolio Value	
Portfolio Communication Management	7.1 Develop Portfolio Communication Management Plan	7.2 Manage Portfolio Information	
Portfolio Risk Management	8.1 Develop Portfolio Risk Management Plan	8.2 Manage Portfolio Risks	

3.1.1 Defining Process Group

The Defining Process Group consists of those processes performed to establish how the organizational strategy and objectives will be implemented in a portfolio; determines the portfolio strategic plan; determines the portfolio structure and roadmap; defines and authorizes a portfolio or subportfolio; and develops the portfolio management plan and subsidiary plans.

The Defining Process Group is most active at the time the organization identifies and updates its strategic goals, near-term budgets, and plans. Traditionally, these activities take place at the annual budgeting time or business review meetings although some organizations have more or less frequent cycles. Such activities could be scheduled quarterly, for example, or may occur because of unscheduled changes in the organization (e.g., mergers, reorganization, changes in enterprise environment factors, etc.).

3.1.2 Aligning Process Group

The Aligning Process Group consists of processes to manage and optimize the portfolio. This group determines how portfolio components will be categorized, evaluated, selected for inclusion, modification, or elimination, and managed in the portfolio. The Aligning Process Group promotes and supports the portfolio based on the strategic goals of the portfolio through the operational rules for evaluating components and building the portfolio. The processes in this Process Group enable the establishment of a structured method for aligning the mix of portfolio components to the organization's strategy.

The Aligning Process Group is most active after the portfolio organization has defined and developed its strategic goals, near-term budgets, and plans. Traditionally, these activities are used to manage ongoing portfolio activities.

3.1.3 Authorizing and Controlling Process Group

The Authorizing and Controlling Process Group consists of the processes for determining how to authorize the portfolio and provides ongoing portfolio oversight. These two processes are central to all the portfolio management processes and are the process steps and activities necessary to enable the portfolio as a whole to perform to achieve metrics defined by the organization.

The authorizing and controlling group determines how to monitor strategic changes; tracks and reviews performance indicators for alignment; and authorizes the portfolio components and verifies values that are delivered to the organization from the portfolio including suggestions and best practices for better strategic planning in the future. These authorizing and oversight processes are the active part of the portfolio and are usually an ongoing function of the organization's governing body.

The portfolio manager often repeats these group and individual constituent processes during the portfolio management process. The Process Groups are not phases, and do not constitute a life cycle. The Process Groups may be repeated for each portfolio or subportfolio.

3.2 Portfolio Management Process Interactions

There is a tight linkage between the Portfolio Management Process Groups and the ongoing organizational process cycle of developing an organizational strategy, aligning all portfolio components to that strategy, and monitoring the results of these decisions. The portfolio management processes act as a series of interrelated processes or bridges between the organizational strategy and the programs/projects that are part of the tactical work to deliver on the goals, objectives, and strategies of the organization. The series of interrelated processes, from the strategy to its effective and efficient execution is a complex series of iterative and continuous processes. These processes accommodate organizational strategy and changes in objectives by revisiting the Aligning processes and providing oversight to all portfolio components.

Figure 3-1 illustrates the relationships between Portfolio Management Process Groups and the organizational strategy and objectives, as well as those organization processes that have an effect on the portfolio management context. Portfolio Management Process Groups also interact with inventory of work and organizational assets, such as portfolio process assets, organizational process assets, and enterprise environmental factors. Figure 3-1 shows that these groups have interdependencies and the portfolio manager utilizes these Process Groups in the management of each portfolio. Constituent processes can also interact, both within their particular Process Group and with the other Portfolio Management Process Groups.

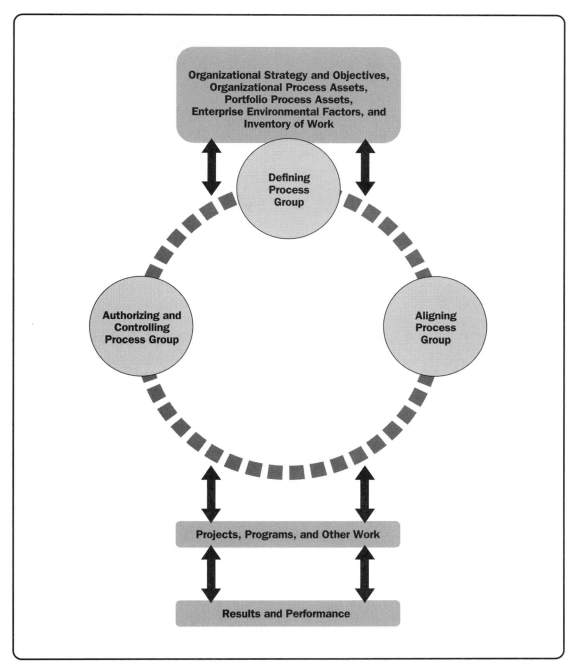

Figure 3-1. Portfolio Management Process Group Interactions

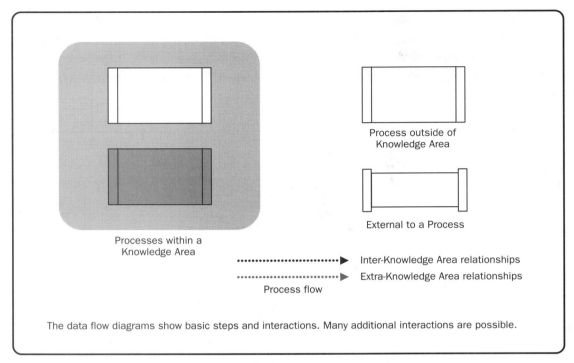

Figure 3-2. Data Flow Diagram Legend

A data flow diagram is provided in each Knowledge Area (Sections 4 through 8). The data flow diagram is a summary level depiction of the process inputs and process outputs that flow down through all the processes within a specific Knowledge Area. Although the processes are presented here as discrete elements with well-defined interfaces, in practice they are iterative and can overlap and interact in ways not detailed here.

The process data flow diagram shown in Figure 3-3 provides an overall summary of the basic flow and interactions among Process Groups, organizational strategy and objectives, organization process context, and the program and project management processes. The process flow diagram illustrates the portfolio management process interactions between the Process Groups, the organization, and the programs, projects, and operations that make up the portfolio components.

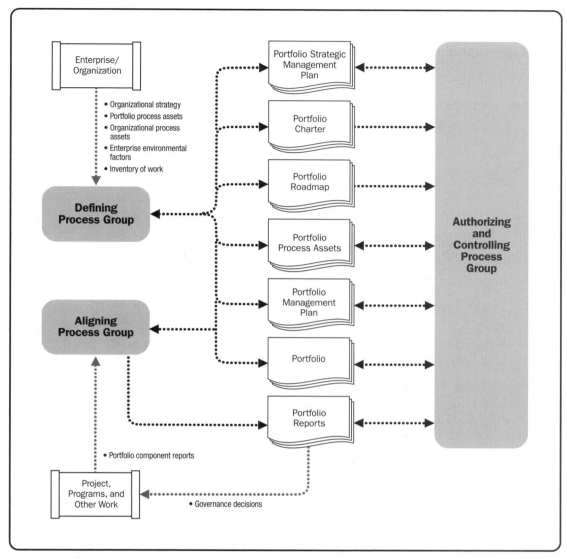

Figure 3-3. Portfolio Management Process Group Interactions

The portfolio risk management practices are the fundamental underlying processes that occur in portfolio management. Risks that arise from the objectives of the portfolio come from a number of areas. They arise in all three Process Groups: Defining, Aligning, and Authorizing and Controlling (see Figure 3-4).

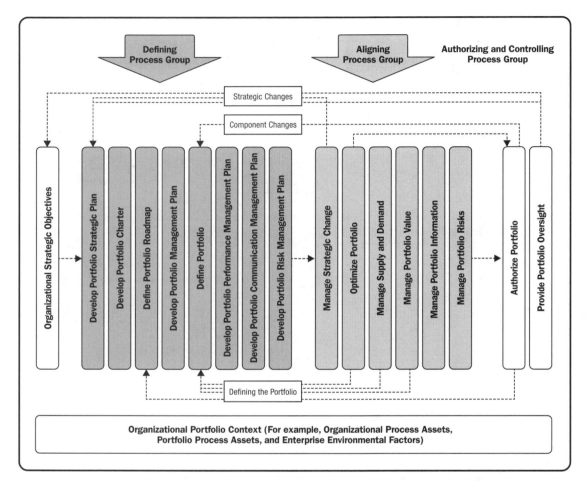

Figure 3-4. Risk Management Processes and the Portfolio Management Process Groups

3.2.1 Common Inputs and Outputs

Common inputs and outputs are those inputs and outputs that are frequently used in multiple portfolio management processes. The multiple uses of common inputs and outputs are one of the factors that make portfolio management complex and nonlinear.

3.2.1.1 Portfolio Process Assets

Portfolio process assets (PPA) include any or all process-related assets, from any of the stakeholders and teams involved in the portfolio that can be used to influence the portfolio's success. These process assets include formal and informal plans, policies, procedures, and guidelines. The process assets also include the portfolio-related knowledge bases, such as lessons learned and historical information. Portfolio process assets may include information on tools, techniques, models, integrated schedules, and risk and performance data. The portfolio manager is generally responsible for updating and adding to the portfolio process assets as necessary, as follows:

- Processes, guidelines, policies, and procedures (e.g., strategic alignment, governance, change management, information distribution, optimization, risk and performance management, etc.);

- Specifications, work instructions, proposal evaluation criteria, and performance measurement criteria;

- Templates (e.g., component proposals, lessons learned, and performance and risk management);

- Portfolio communication requirements (e.g., specific communication technology available, allowed communication media, record retention policies, and security requirements);

- Procedures for portfolio component work authorizations;

- Performance measurement databases used to collect and make available measurement data on portfolio components and track cash flow, including actual resources used and forecast of resources required;

- Portfolio component files (e.g., component proposals, investments, performance measurement baselines, calendars, risk registers); and

- Historical information and lessons learned knowledge bases (e.g., portfolio records and documents, portfolio component closure information and documentation, information about both the results of previous portfolio selection decisions and previous portfolio performance information and information from the risk management effort).

3.2.1.2 Portfolio Reports

Portfolio reports may include, but are not limited to the following:

- Performance reports, including scorecards and dashboards,
- Feedback report to organizational strategy planning,
- Variance reports,
- Resource capacity and capability reports,
- Portfolio risks and issues,
- Governance recommendations,
- Governance decisions, and
- Portfolio component recommendations.

3.2.1.3 Organizational Process Assets

Organizational process assets are the plans, processes, policies, procedures, and knowledge bases, specific to and used by the performing organization, that can be leveraged by the portfolio manager.

3.2.1.4 Enterprise Environmental Factors

Enterprise environmental factors refer to internal or external conditions, not under the control of the portfolio organization, which influence, constrain, or direct a portfolio's success. These factors occur externally to the portfolio organization and outside of its direct control, yet they impact the portfolio management decision processes.

Enterprise environmental factors may constrain portfolio management options and may have a positive or negative influence on the outcome. Enterprise environmental factors include, but are not limited to:

- Organizational governance processes, culture, and detailed hierarchy structure;
- Legal constraints;
- Governmental or industry standards (e.g., regulatory agency regulations, codes of conduct, product standards, quality standards, and workmanship standards);
- Infrastructure (e.g., existing facilities and capital equipment);
- Existing human resources (e.g., skills, disciplines, and knowledge, such as design, development, law, contracting, and purchasing);
- Personnel administration (e.g., hiring and firing guidelines, employee performance reviews, and training records);
- Marketplace conditions;
- Portfolio management information system (i.e., tools, manual or automated, for information collection and distribution to support the portfolio management processes);
- Commercial databases (e.g., standardized cost estimating data, industry risk study, and information and risk databases);
- Organizational project management; and
- Stakeholder risk tolerances.

3.2.2 Key Deliverables Across Portfolio Management Processes

There are six key deliverables that are needed for the portfolio management processes. Table 3-2 describes each of these documents, their purpose, and the contents. The six deliverables are:

- Portfolio strategic plan,
- Portfolio charter,
- Portfolio management plan,
- Portfolio roadmap, and
- Portfolio.

Table 3-2. Key Deliverables for Portfolio Management Processes

KEY DELIVERABLE	PURPOSE	CONTENT
Portfolio Strategic Plan	The portfolio strategic plan articulates the options, preferences, and factors that will be considered in a specific portfolio that will aid the decision makers in aligning, authorizing and controlling the portfolio and its individual components with the organizational strategy, future benefit, and stakeholder expectations. Preexisting portfolios or inventories of work should be validated against organizational strategy updates to ensure consistency with the evolving organizational mission, goals, and objectives. Thus, by comparing new and preexisting components with/against one another, it may be determined that it is preferable to add, modify, or divest some components to ensure the portfolio objectives are aligned with the strategic plan.	Vision for the portfolio, which is based on the alignment with the organization's goals and objectives
		Allocation of funds and resources for different types of initiatives (portfolios, subportfolios, and other work) and how these contribute to the organization's objectives
		Portfolio benefits are clearly and consistently identified
		Initiatives can be appraised and prioritized
		Strategic objectives can be optimized with available resources and risks
		Key assumptions, constraints, dependencies, and risks
		Portfolio structure including a listing of the various portfolio components and other work
		Portfolio prioritization model
Portfolio Charter	The portfolio charter is the document that formally authorizes and structures a portfolio. The charter provides the portfolio manager with the authority to apply portfolio resources to projects and other work within the portfolio. Chartering a portfolio links the portfolio to the organizational strategic plan and describes how the portfolio will deliver value to the organization.	The portfolio charter should include the portfolio vision, high-level scope, justification, success criteria, resources, and high-level timelines for portfolio delivery
		Identification of stakeholders
Portfolio Management Plan	The portfolio management plan describes the approach and intent of management in identifying, approving, procuring, prioritizing, balancing, managing, and reporting a portfolio of programs, projects, and other work to meet the organization's strategic objectives.	Governance model
		Portfolio oversight
		Managing strategic changes
		Change control and management
		Balancing portfolio and managing dependencies
		Measuring and monitoring performance and value
		Portfolio performance reporting and review
		Communication model as part of the communication management plan
		Portfolio risk management planning
		Procurement procedures
		Managing compliance
		Portfolio prioritization model
Portfolio Roadmap	The portfolio roadmap provides the high-level strategic direction and information in a chronological fashion for portfolio management execution and ensures that dependencies within the portfolio are established and evaluated.	List of components
	The roadmap can be considered to be the high-level prioritization mapping of the portfolio over time, and the crucial aspect of the roadmap is that it forms the initial basis upon which dependencies are established both within the portfolio and externally so they can then be tracked.	Dependencies
		Key milestones and deliverables
Portfolio	A portfolio is a collection of projects, programs, and/or other work that are adopted and grouped together to facilitate the effective management of that work to meet strategic business objectives. The projects, programs, and/or other work may not necessarily be interdependent or directly related. The portfolio and its components are quantifiable; that is, they can be measured, ranked, and prioritized.	List of components with attributes (including but not limited to: costs, time, resources, velocity of the component's completion, etc.) and portfolio structure

3

PORTFOLIO STRATEGIC MANAGEMENT

Portfolio Strategic Management includes the processes to develop the portfolio strategic plan, the portfolio charter, and the portfolio roadmap and to assess and manage the alignment of these three deliverables to the organizational strategy and objectives. In addition, portfolio strategic management involves managing, monitoring, and responding to ongoing changes in organizational strategy and in portfolio components to determine appropriate actions. Actions may include a modification to strategy and goals or changes to the portfolio itself.

The Portfolio Strategic Management processes are (see Figure 4-1 for overview):

4.1 Develop Portfolio Strategic Plan.—Evaluating the high-level organization strategy/investment decisions and defining the strategy in portfolio-related strategic goals and objectives in the portfolio strategic plan.

4.2 Develop Portfolio Charter.—Creating the portfolio charter and identifying the portfolio structure and portfolio management team (if applicable) to align with the portfolio strategic plan.

4.3 Define Portfolio Roadmap.—Creating a high-level schedule showing the strategic plan for components to be implemented over time with any dependencies between them so that management may evaluate any conflicts or gaps between the roadmap and the organizational strategy and objectives.

4.4 Manage Strategic Change.—Evaluating and determining the responses to ongoing changes in organization strategy or portfolio components, and updating the portfolio management plan and subsidiary plans to reflect the impacts and response for portfolio management processes.

4.1 Develop Portfolio Strategic Plan

The Develop Portfolio Strategic Plan process consists of developing a portfolio strategic plan and aligning the strategic management of the portfolio to the organizational strategy and objectives. The portfolio is aligned to the organizational strategy and objectives for the corporate, organization unit, functional, or department level, based on portfolio management objectives, prioritization, allocation of funds, organizational benefits, performance expectations, resources, assumptions, constraints, dependencies, risks, and requirements. Figure 4-2 shows the inputs, tools and techniques, and outputs. Figure 4-3 shows the data flow diagram.

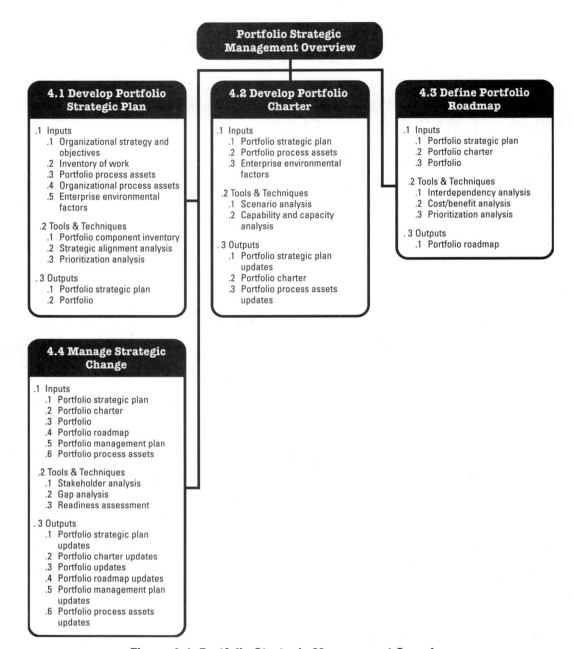

4.1 Develop Portfolio Strategic Plan

.1 Inputs
  .1 Organizational strategy and objectives
  .2 Inventory of work
  .3 Portfolio process assets
  .4 Organizational process assets
  .5 Enterprise environmental factors

.2 Tools & Techniques
  .1 Portfolio component inventory
  .2 Strategic alignment analysis
  .3 Prioritization analysis

.3 Outputs
  .1 Portfolio strategic plan
  .2 Portfolio

4.2 Develop Portfolio Charter

.1 Inputs
  .1 Portfolio strategic plan
  .2 Portfolio process assets
  .3 Enterprise environmental factors

.2 Tools & Techniques
  .1 Scenario analysis
  .2 Capability and capacity analysis

.3 Outputs
  .1 Portfolio strategic plan updates
  .2 Portfolio charter
  .3 Portfolio process assets updates

4.3 Define Portfolio Roadmap

.1 Inputs
  .1 Portfolio strategic plan
  .2 Portfolio charter
  .3 Portfolio

.2 Tools & Techniques
  .1 Interdependency analysis
  .2 Cost/benefit analysis
  .3 Prioritization analysis

.3 Outputs
  .1 Portfolio roadmap

4.4 Manage Strategic Change

.1 Inputs
  .1 Portfolio strategic plan
  .2 Portfolio charter
  .3 Portfolio
  .4 Portfolio roadmap
  .5 Portfolio management plan
  .6 Portfolio process assets

.2 Tools & Techniques
  .1 Stakeholder analysis
  .2 Gap analysis
  .3 Readiness assessment

.3 Outputs
  .1 Portfolio strategic plan updates
  .2 Portfolio charter updates
  .3 Portfolio updates
  .4 Portfolio roadmap updates
  .5 Portfolio management plan updates
  .6 Portfolio process assets updates

Figure 4-1. Portfolio Strategic Management Overview

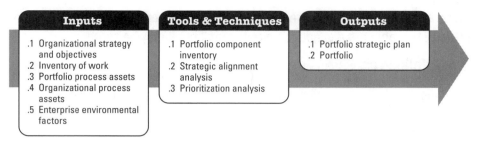

Figure 4-2. Develop Portfolio Strategic Plan: Inputs, Tools and Techniques, and Outputs

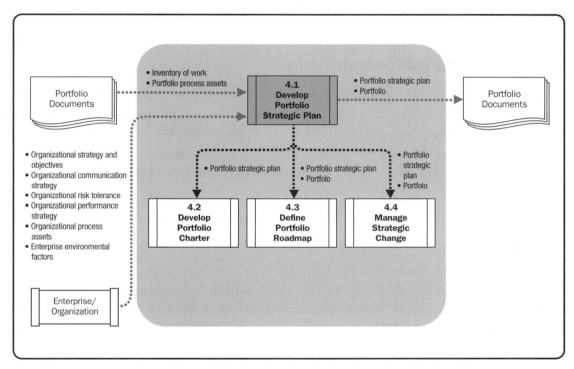

Figure 4-3. Develop Portfolio Strategic Plan: Data Flow Diagram

4.1.1   Develop Portfolio Strategic Plan: Inputs

4.1.1.1   Organizational Strategy and Objectives

Organizational strategy and objectives provide long-term direction, vision, goals, and objectives. This input may also take the form of a document that contains the mission, vision, strategy, and objectives with various levels of detail depending upon the purpose and scope of the plan within the organization.

4.1.1.2   Inventory of Work

At a minimum an organization should have an inventory of work to serve as a starting point for developing a portfolio. The organization may also have a prioritization of these portfolio components. The portfolio may be progressively elaborated as more details are gathered on its components. The list of portfolio components or inventory of work may be immature and not optimized or final but it may be evolving.

4.1.1.3   Portfolio Process Assets

During the alignment of the organizational strategy and objectives, the portfolio manager references and is guided by the portfolio's plans, policies, procedures, and guidelines. Various tools and templates may be utilized such as benefits analysis and reporting. Portfolio process assets are described in Section 3.

4.1.1.4   Organizational Process Assets

Organizational process assets may influence the Develop Portfolio Strategic Plan process. These organizational process assets may provide information and direction about the organizational strategy and objectives, vision and mission statements, prioritization, and resources. Organizational process assets are described in Section 3.

4.1.1.5   Enterprise Environmental Factors

Enterprise environmental factors described in Section 3 may consist of corporate, environmental, and governmental variables that contribute to the Develop Portfolio Strategic Plan process. EEFs influence the organizational strategy and objectives and may also impact the Develop Portfolio Strategic Plan process, particularly factors such as organizational structure, stakeholder risk tolerances, marketplace conditions, and human resources. Knowledge of these factors and their impacts may be context for and included in the portfolio strategic plan.

4.1.2   Develop Portfolio Strategic Plan: Tools and Techniques

Organizational strategy and objectives are analyzed to determine which part of the portfolio structure will address specific organization strategy. The current inventory of work or existing portfolio should be analyzed to determine which portfolio component will be continued, modified, or discontinued and whether any new components should be added. The techniques should include the analysis of the drivers of strategic change to determine the desired contribution of the initiatives to the strategic objectives.

4.1.2.1   Portfolio Component Inventory

By understanding the objectives, expected benefits, performance, and prioritization criteria, the portfolio manager is able to define the portfolio in accordance with strategic direction and prioritization criteria. This may be an initial portfolio based on a list of work, and the portfolio may be further elaborated to reduce gaps in meeting strategic objectives.

4.1.2.2   Strategic Alignment Analysis

The strategic alignment analysis focuses on the new or changing organizational strategy and objectives. The analysis also indicates where there are gaps in focus, investment, or alignment within the portfolio.

Portfolios or inventory of work must be validated against organizational strategy updates to ensure consistency with the evolving organizational mission, goals, and objectives. Thus, by comparing new components to preexisting components, the portfolio manager should be able to determine whether it is preferable to add, modify, or terminate some components to ensure the portfolio objectives remain aligned with the organizational strategy and objectives. Factors that may indicate a need for a revision of the portfolio components include: obsolete goals, opportunities to be pursued, and response to regulatory changes, etc. Results of the analysis become part of the portfolio process assets.

Figure 4-4 displays a structure according to a high-level timeline. The various organization areas are indicated with the as-is situation and to-be vision indicated at either end of the spectrum. The boxes refer to multiple portfolio components in the various organization areas. It provides an integrated view of the overall portfolio strategy and demonstrates one type of tool that can be used as a step in conducting strategic alignment analysis. After mapping the schedule, the analysis moves to identifying dependencies and potential conflicts in the plan.

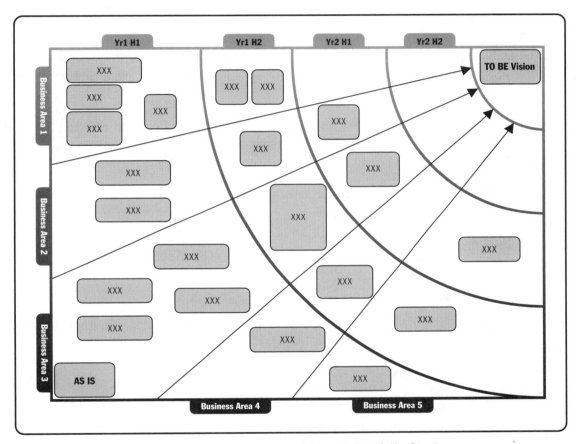

Figure 4-4. Integrated View of Overall Portfolio Strategy

4.1.2.3   Prioritization Analysis

The portfolio strategic plan should contain a prioritization model or approach that guides the ongoing decisions as to which portfolio components should be added, terminated, or changed, as well as prioritizes and balances the component mix over time.

A simple prioritization model may be provided which contains criteria to ensure alignment to strategic goals, expected return on investment (ROI), investment risks, and dependencies. Scoring elements may be based on strategic alignment, financial benefits, financial costs, risk, and dependencies to determine an overall scoring and ranking.

Based on the measurement for each criterion, portfolio components are scored and compared to assist in establishing the portfolio and are used when evaluating the portfolio throughout its life cycle.

There are various tools, techniques, and models to assist in performing prioritization analyses. Some examples are weighted ranking and scoring techniques as described in Section 5.2.

4.1.3 Develop Portfolio Strategic Plan: Outputs

4.1.3.1 Portfolio Strategic Plan

The portfolio strategic plan should be produced using the organizational strategy and objectives. The portfolio manager should collaborate with management in the governing bodies and key stakeholders in the development of the plan. The portfolio strategic plan may address the organizational strategy for the corporate, organization unit, functional or department level. The relationship between portfolio management and organizational strategy is described in Section 1.5.

Organizational strategy is implemented through portfolio components and ongoing operations. In producing the portfolio strategic plan, the portfolio manager should integrate and respond to changes in the portfolio while remaining aligned with the organizational strategy and objectives.

To create the portfolio strategic plan, the portfolio vision and objectives are defined to align with organizational strategy. The portfolio strategic plan key contents are:

- Portfolio vision and objectives;
- Organizational structure and organization areas;
- Measurable goals and guidance;
- Allocation of funds to different types of initiatives (portfolios, subportfolios) and how these contribute to the organizational strategy and objectives;
- Portfolio benefits, performance results, and value expected;
- Communication required to ensure successful change and implementation;
- Key assumptions, constraints, dependencies, and risks;
- Resources required by type and quantity;
- Portfolio prioritization model, a high-level prioritization, decision-making framework; and
- Risk tolerance.

4.1.3.2 Portfolio

The portfolio is the updated list of components resulting from developing a strategic plan and aligning identified work or components to the defined organizational strategy and objectives. When just beginning a portfolio from an inventory of work, the portfolio may evolve as more details are obtained such as dependencies, timelines, and strategic changes resulting from both internal and external forces.

4.2 Develop Portfolio Charter

During the Develop Portfolio Charter process, the portfolio charter is created and the portfolio structure is defined. The portfolio charter is produced through this process to authorize the portfolio manager to apply portfolio resources to portfolio components and to execute the portfolio management processes. The structure is developed based on strategies and priorities, and portfolio components are grouped to facilitate effective management. The structure identifies the portfolio, subportfolios, programs, and projects based on organization areas included, hierarchies, timelines, and goals for each program, project, and operation to align with the portfolio strategic plan. Once the structure is defined, updates will be needed to the strategic management plan and portfolio process assets to ensure goals and standards alignment. Figure 4-5 shows the inputs, tools and techniques, and outputs. Figure 4-6 shows the data flow diagram.

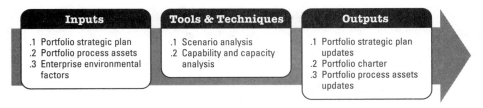

Inputs	Tools & Techniques	Outputs
.1 Portfolio strategic plan .2 Portfolio process assets .3 Enterprise environmental factors	.1 Scenario analysis .2 Capability and capacity analysis	.1 Portfolio strategic plan updates .2 Portfolio charter .3 Portfolio process assets updates

Figure 4-5. Develop Portfolio Charter: Inputs, Tools and Techniques, and Outputs

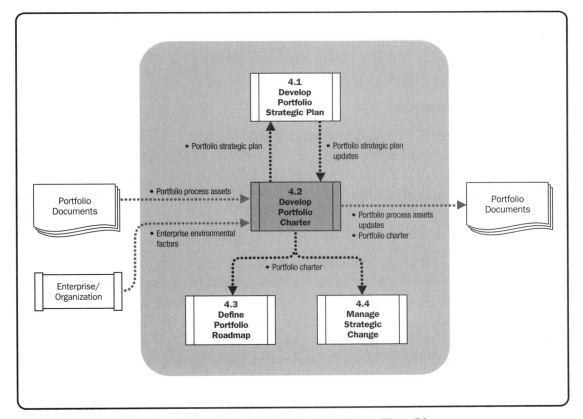

Figure 4-6. Develop Portfolio Charter: Data Flow Diagram

4.2.1 Develop Portfolio Charter: Inputs

4.2.1.1 Portfolio Strategic Plan

When developing the portfolio charter and defining the portfolio structure, it is important to *be guided by* the portfolio strategic plan, as described in Section 4.1. The information in the portfolio strategic plan necessary for developing the portfolio charter is the portfolio vision and objectives, the benefits expected, and the key risks, dependencies, and constraints.

Within the portfolio strategic plan, the prioritization model is useful as a decision framework to structure the portfolio components.

4.2.1.2 Portfolio Process Assets

To develop the portfolio charter, the portfolio manager should leverage the portfolio's plans, policies, procedures, and guidelines, and any existing documentation of stakeholder relationships, scope, benefits, and portfolio goals. Portfolio process assets are described in Section 3.

4.2.1.3 Enterprise Environmental Factors

Enterprise environmental factors as described in Section 3 may consist of corporate, environmental and governmental variables that may contribute to and constrain the Develop Portfolio Charter process. The portfolio structure in the charter may need to align with corporate accounting structure or with the functional structure of the organization (e.g., by organization unit or department).

4.2.2 Develop Portfolio Charter: Tools and Techniques

4.2.2.1 Scenario Analysis

This analytical method enables decision makers to create a variety of portfolio scenarios using different combinations of both potential components and current components, evaluating their possible outcomes based on various assumptions. The result of this analysis allows decision makers to determine the portfolio structure and objectives for inclusion in the portfolio charter.

4.2.2.2 Capability and Capacity Analysis

Capability and capacity analysis is performed to understand how much work is able to be performed based on the resources available (capacity), as well as the ability of the organization to source and execute the selected portfolio and to determine the constraints generated by certain skill set limitations, financial constraints, and other asset capacity factors (capability). Internal resource capacity is required to be measured and external resource availability is required to be established to complete the portfolio structure. These human resource, financial, and asset capacity considerations will be limiting factors for the number and size of portfolio components the organization can execute. Capability and capacity analysis is further described in Section 5.3.2.

4.2.3 Develop Portfolio Charter: Outputs

4.2.3.1 Portfolio Strategic Plan Updates

The portfolio strategic plan is updated to reflect resulting changes from defining the portfolio structure. Some examples of updates and changes to the plan may include changes in organization areas, updates to the organizational structure of the portfolio as well as updates in relationships, dependencies, and goals of the portfolio components.

4.2.3.2 Portfolio Charter

A portfolio charter is the document that formally authorizes the portfolio manager to apply portfolio resources to the portfolio component. The charter provides the portfolio structure including the hierarchy and organization of the portfolio, subportfolios, programs, projects, and operations and forecasts how and when the portfolio will deliver value to the organization. Chartering a portfolio links the portfolio to the organizational strategy and describes how the portfolio will deliver value to the organization. The charter may include portfolio objectives, portfolio justification, portfolio sponsor(s), portfolio management roles and responsibilities, key and major stakeholders, stakeholder expectations and requirements, communication requirements, high-level scope, benefits, critical success criteria, resources, high-level timeline, and assumptions, constraints, dependencies, and risks.

4.2.3.3 Portfolio Process Asset Updates

Portfolio process assets include formal and informal plans, policies, procedures, and guidelines, which may need to be updated. The portfolio structure itself may be considered a guideline to identify the portfolio and subportfolios based on organization areas, hierarchies, and goals for each portfolio component.

4.3 Define Portfolio Roadmap

Portfolio roadmaps are an output of high-level portfolio planning that graphically depicts all portfolio elements needed to achieve organizational strategy and objectives. The roadmap provides a high level plan which should then be used for identifying both internal and external dependencies. The portfolio roadmaps may contain both program level and project level roadmaps included in the scope of the portfolio. Roadmaps may not provide details of all identified portfolio components at the onset, however, they may be used to build details later. Figure 4-7 shows the inputs, tools and techniques, and outputs. Figure 4-8 shows the data flow diagram.

Inputs	Tools & Techniques	Outputs
.1 Portfolio strategic plan .2 Portfolio charter .3 Portfolio	.1 Interdependency analysis .2 Cost-benefit analysis .3 Prioritization analysis	.1 Portfolio roadmap

Figure 4-7. Define Portfolio Roadmap: Inputs, Tools and Techniques, and Outputs

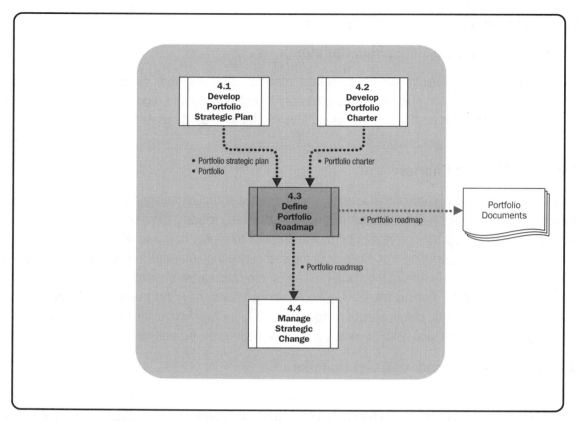

Figure 4-8. Define Portfolio Roadmap: Data Flow Diagram

The roadmap shows alignment from the components to the strategic objectives or highlights the gaps between the components and the strategic objectives that need to be analyzed. In addition, it supports mapping of portfolio milestones and dependencies, and identifies the challenges and risks. It can be used to communicate the linkage between the organization strategy and portfolio management and is used by the governance processes to determine when new components should be initiated.

The roadmap can also provide a high-level prioritization mapping of the portfolio over time. The roadmap forms the initial basis on which dependencies are established both within the portfolio and externally so they can then be tracked. External dependencies are those dependencies between organization areas, which are outside of the portfolio.

4.3.1 Define Portfolio Roadmap: Inputs

4.3.1.1 Portfolio Strategic Plan

The portfolio strategic plan will reflect the organizational goals, objectives, and strategies necessary to enable alignment of the portfolio roadmap. The portfolio strategic plan provides the portfolio prioritization model that establishes the guidelines to prioritize portfolio components, enabling the portfolio roadmap to be built.

4.3.1.2 Portfolio Charter

The portfolio charter is needed to understand the portfolio structure, scope, constraints, dependencies, resources, and high-level timeline in order to create the portfolio roadmap.

4.3.1.3 Portfolio

The portfolio components and related information should be referenced to define the portfolio roadmap. Examples of information referenced are prioritization, dependencies, and organization areas.

4.3.2 Define Portfolio Roadmap: Tools and Techniques

4.3.2.1 Interdependency Analysis

The interdependency analysis should identify the dependencies the portfolio may have in relationship to other portfolios or to the portfolio environment. Dependencies to be analyzed may include resources, finance, quality, risks, timelines, etc. Participants in this analysis may include executive level and other key stakeholders.

4.3.2.2 Cost-Benefit Analysis

The cost-benefit analysis quantifies estimated costs and benefits and lists qualitative considerations of alternative portfolio components for evaluation in determining the best course of action.

4.3.2.3 Prioritization Analysis

To accomplish the prioritization analysis, the portfolio manager should compare strategic objectives, prioritize objectives, and perform strategic assessment against current enterprise portfolios.

4.3.3 Define Portfolio Roadmap: Outputs

4.3.3.1 Portfolio Roadmap

The portfolio roadmap should provide the high-level strategic direction and information in a chronological view for portfolio management execution and enable dependencies within the portfolio to be established and evaluated. In the example in Figure 4-9, the high-level timeline appears across the top of the structure, and the portfolio components are listed in the first column.

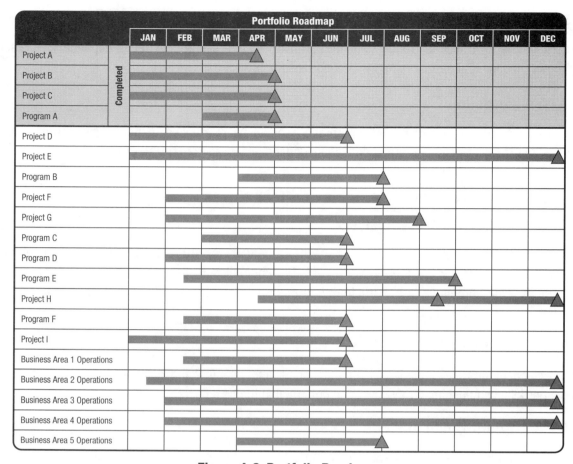

Figure 4-9. Portfolio Roadmap

4.4 Manage Strategic Change

The Manage Strategic Change process enables the portfolio manager to manage changes in organizational strategy and to enhance the ability to accept and act on significant strategic change that impacts portfolio planning and management.

As strategy shifts, the "as-is" state must be compared with the "to-be" state (which may be evolutionary or incremental in nature), and a gap may result in a realignment of resources or adjustments in the portfolio component mix to support the strategic change. Change in portfolios is a normal occurrence, and, depending on the significance of the changes, portfolio documents may need to be reworked to ensure continued alignment with the strategy. This repeated adaptation is in contrast to the progressive elaboration required in project management. This process is an aligning process to identify the gap between as-is and to-be states and to analyze the impact and response to strategic changes and changes in resources (people, processes, and assets/technology). The vehicles used to plan and execute the strategic change are the portfolio strategic plan and portfolio management plan. Figure 4-10 shows the inputs, tools and techniques, and outputs. Figure 4-11 shows the data flow diagram.

Figure 4-10. Manage Strategic Change: Inputs, Tools and Techniques, and Outputs

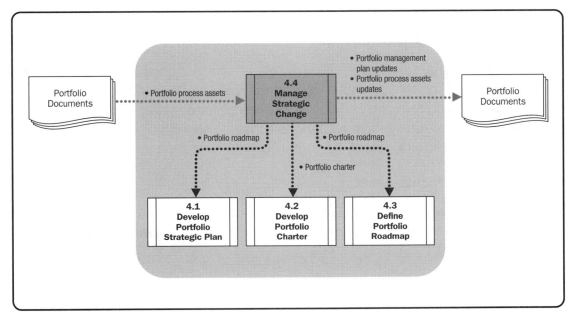

Figure 4-11. Manage Strategic Change: Data Flow Diagram

4.4.1   Manage Strategic Change: Inputs

4.4.1.1   Portfolio Strategic Plan

The portfolio strategic plan is described in Section 4.1.3.1. When managing strategic change, it is important to understand the portfolio strategic plan in order to ensure inclusion of the correct components within those organization areas with the highest strategic value. Due to new strategic direction, before and during the portfolio changes, the executives' and key stakeholders' expectations and communication requirements need to be considered.

4.4.1.2   Portfolio Charter

The portfolio charter is described in Section 4.2.3.2. In managing strategic change, the original portfolio charter or revised charter, if applicable, should be reviewed to ensure the charter and portfolio remain in alignment and are updated as required.

4.4.1.3 Portfolio

The portfolio is the means to the "to-be" vision. The list of current portfolio components are reviewed and evaluated to determine the required changes in the component mix and to align with the strategic direction.

4.4.1.4 Portfolio Roadmap

The portfolio roadmap provides the high-level strategic approach in a chronological fashion for portfolio management execution and ensures that dependencies within the portfolio are established and evaluated. This is an essential component in enabling management of the portfolio and demonstrating a clear path from the "as-is" to the "to-be" states. Reviewing or updating the portfolio roadmap ensures that it is in sync with changes in strategic direction.

4.4.1.5 Portfolio Management Plan

The portfolio management plan provides portfolio oversight with the format and planned criteria for developing, maintaining, and controlling the portfolio and its components. The plan documents the intended approach to managing the portfolio and its components in order to meet the organization strategy and objectives. In managing strategic change, the portfolio management plan should be reassessed and, if necessary, updated to ensure probable mission success based on the updated strategy.

4.4.1.6 Portfolio Process Assets

Portfolio process assets are described in Section 3. In managing strategic change, the portfolio manager references and is guided by the portfolio's plans, policies, procedures, and guidelines. Examples of assets may include analysis and assessment tools and templates.

4.4.2 Manage Strategic Change: Tools and Techniques

4.4.2.1 Stakeholder Analysis

Stakeholder analysis is critical in managing strategic change because it helps to ensure continuity and align key stakeholders' expectations with the changing strategy and resulting portfolio realignment. The techniques used to analyze stakeholder expectations and requirements may include interviewing senior executive stakeholders and analyzing requirements and expectations for strategic change. This may include identifying the stakeholders by individual or group, determining expectations, evolving conditions, newly recognized pain points, problems or desires, change impacts, issues, risk tolerance, and concerns.

4.4.2.2 Gap Analysis

A gap analysis is performed to compare the current portfolio mix and components with the new strategic direction and the "to-be" organizational vision. This is essential to properly manage strategic change. This analysis determines the gaps and changes needed in the portfolio mix in order that components may be added, changed, or terminated.

4.4.2.3   Readiness Assessment

A readiness assessment is performed to assess how ready the organization is to perform the steps necessary to bridge the gap between the "as-is" portfolio state and the "to-be" state. The assessment determines the *if*, *when*, *what*, and *how* of implementing the change, and points out any needs not yet addressed that are required in order to affect the change.

4.4.3   Manage Strategic Change: Outputs

4.4.3.1   Portfolio Strategic Plan Updates

The portfolio strategic plan is updated to reflect the outcome of the tools and techniques listed in 4.4.2 and will need to be revisited when future strategic changes are made. Various elements of the portfolio strategic plan may need to change to reflect the organizational strategy change such as the prioritization model, benefits, assumptions, constraints, dependencies, and risks.

4.4.3.2   Portfolio Charter Updates

The portfolio charter is updated to reflect the outcome of the tools and techniques listed in 4.4.2 and revisited when future strategic changes are made. The portfolio structure in the charter may need to change to reflect new strategic objectives, as well as key or major stakeholders and their communication requirements.

4.4.3.3   Portfolio Updates

When a strategic change is made, components may be added, delayed, or removed from the portfolio to enable alignment with the new strategy.

4.4.3.4   Portfolio Roadmap Updates

Based on the impact of the strategic change, the portfolio roadmap is updated taking into consideration the new "to-be" vision and resulting changes in the portfolio components, timeline, and dependencies.

4.4.3.5   Portfolio Management Plan Updates

Portfolio management plan updates may be needed due to changes in management approach, priorities, organizational structure, and other aspects of the portfolio management plan which may result from the strategic change. Updates to the stakeholder engagement, communication management, performance, and risk sections may be required also as a result of the stakeholder, gap, and readiness assessments.

4.4.3.6   Portfolio Process Assets Updates

If strategic changes impact portfolio plans and processes, the portfolio process assets are updated. These assets include information available from historic files on previous strategic change to the portfolio-related people, processes, and technology, performance metrics, risk management, and lessons learned databases.

5

PORTFOLIO GOVERNANCE MANAGEMENT

The Portfolio Governance Management Knowledge Area processes include portfolio oversight and how to plan for, define, optimize, and authorize the portfolio in support of overall governance body decision-making activities. Portfolio governance management ensures that investment analysis is done to identify opportunities and threats; to assess changes, dependencies, and impact; to select, prioritize, and schedule activities to fund; and to achieve performance targets.

The Portfolio Governance Management processes are (see Figure 5-1 for overview):

5.1 Develop Portfolio Management Plan—Defining portfolio components, developing the portfolio management organization structure, and creating the portfolio management plan.

5.2 Define Portfolio—Creating qualified portfolio components and organizing them for ongoing evaluation, selection, and prioritization.

5.3 Optimize Portfolio—Reviewing, analyzing, and changing portfolio components to create the optimal balance to achieve the organizational strategy and objectives.

5.4 Authorize Portfolio—Allocating resources to develop component proposals, authorizing components to expend resources and to communicate portfolio decisions.

5.5 Provide Portfolio Oversight—Monitoring the portfolio to ensure alignment with the organizational strategy and objectives; making governance decisions in response to portfolio performance, portfolio component changes, and issues and risks to ensure the delivery of the portfolio is in line with the portfolio roadmap, current progress, and conditions (including resources).

5.1 Develop Portfolio Management Plan

The Develop Portfolio Management Plan process consists of developing and updating the portfolio management plan to ensure alignment with the portfolio strategic plan objectives, the portfolio charter authorization, and the portfolio roadmap. Portfolio management plan development is an iterative process and includes the integration of subsidiary plans such as performance, communication, and risk management plans. This collection of plans may be developed concurrently or separately. The portfolio management plan establishes how a portfolio is defined, organized, optimized, and controlled. Figure 5-2 shows the inputs, tools and techniques, and outputs. Figure 5-3 shows the data flow diagram.

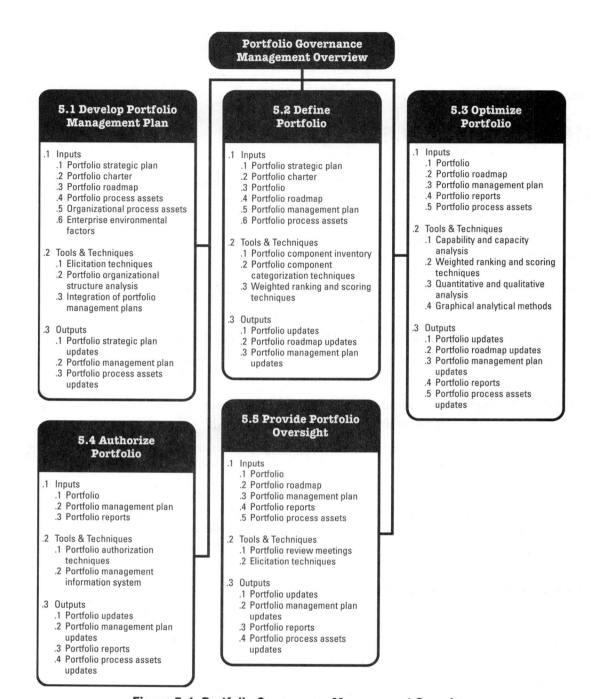

Figure 5-1. Portfolio Governance Management Overview

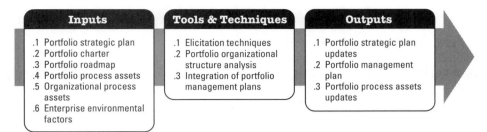

Figure 5-2. Develop Portfolio Management Plan: Inputs, Tools and Techniques, and Outputs

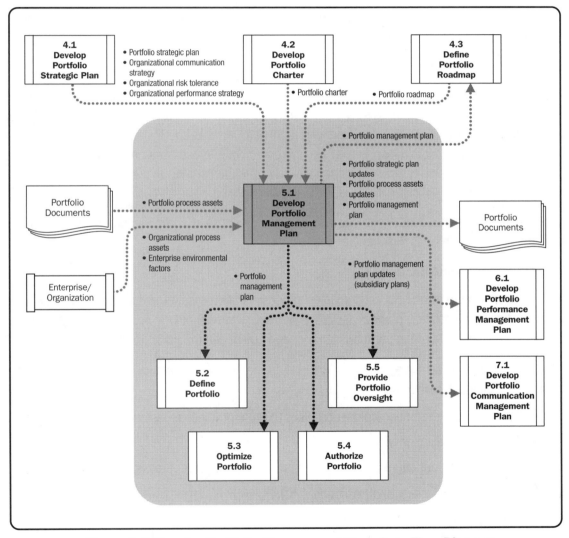

Figure 5-3. Develop Portfolio Management Plan: Data Flow Diagram

5.1.1 Develop Portfolio Management Plan: Inputs

5.1.1.1 Portfolio Strategic Plan

When developing the portfolio management plan, it is important to be guided by the portfolio strategic plan. The portfolio strategic plan provides specifically the organizational risk tolerance, the organizational communication strategy, and the organizational performance strategy. In addition, the portfolio strategic plan has the portfolio objectives, portfolio management organizational structure, benefits, prioritization model, and resource information. The portfolio strategic plan is described in Section 4.1.3.1.

5.1.1.2 Portfolio Charter

The portfolio charter is required to create the portfolio management plan and to understand the portfolio structure, portfolio scope, resources, timeline, stakeholder communication requirements, performance expectations, and key risks, dependencies, and constraints. The portfolio charter is described in Section 4.2.3.2.

5.1.1.3 Portfolio Roadmap

The portfolio management plan utilizes information from the portfolio roadmap's high-level strategic direction and extended timelines to define the low-level schedule and timelines for portfolio components. This approach of managing the portfolio ensures the dependencies between portfolio components as defined in the portfolio roadmap are met. For instance, the dependencies and integration of portfolio components as defined in the portfolio roadmap influence the approach to communication and risk management in the portfolio management plan.

The portfolio management plan may describe or refer to different methodologies or approaches which the organization applies to manage different classes or types of portfolio components, specified in the portfolio roadmap. The portfolio roadmap is described in Section 4.3.3.1.

5.1.1.4 Portfolio Process Assets

Portfolio process assets include portfolio policies, processes and procedures, and portfolio knowledge bases. Updating and adding to the portfolio process assets, as necessary throughout the portfolio management processes, are generally the responsibility of the portfolio manager and outlined in the portfolio management plan.

Also portfolio process assets may include current information which should be used to establish portfolio management processes and define responsibilities:

- Performance information from a portfolio's past performance or history (for benchmarking purposes),
- Portfolio management decisions and open issues, and
- Information about ongoing and planned portfolio management tasks.

Portfolio process assets are described in Section 3.1.2.1.

5.1.1.5 Organizational Process Assets

Organizational process assets include organizational processes, procedures, and knowledge bases. These assets can be referenced when developing the portfolio management plan and developing the portfolio management approach. Organizational process assets are described in Section 3.1.2.3.

5.1.1.6 Enterprise Environmental Factors

Enterprise environmental factors (EEFs) include the organization's overall governance processes and may consist of corporate, environmental, and governmental variables that can contribute to the determination of how to manage certain aspects of a portfolio. The portfolio management plan establishes processes to monitor specific EEFs and their critical values which can switch on specific portfolio management processes (escalations, change requests, portfolio management process improvements, etc.). Enterprise environmental factors are described in Section 3.1.2.4.

5.1.2 Develop Portfolio Management Plan: Tools and Techniques

5.1.2.1 Elicitation Techniques

The portfolio manager elicits requirements for the portfolio management plan from a variety of sources and in a variety of ways. The benefit of using elicitation techniques for the portfolio management plan is greatest in the portfolio development (discovery). These techniques can target the oversight team, key stakeholders, working groups, or subject matter experts. Some of the methods used to elicit key information may include the following:

- **Facilitation techniques.** These include focus groups and brainstorming activities. During these facilitated sessions, a mind-map diagram may be used as one type of tool to organize the ideas from stakeholders into logical groupings for consideration and incorporation into the plan.

- **Survey techniques.** These include the use of interview and observation survey techniques to capture stakeholder input.

- **Collaboration techniques.** These techniques can be employed to ensure that the plan has the benefit of polling input from a team as a consensus or majority vote. Votes can be sought electronically and often anonymously; then reports can be generated to display popular opinion on recommended scope changes. The benefit of using elicitation techniques for the portfolio management plan is greatest in the portfolio development stages and before implementing significant scope changes. These techniques can target the oversight team, key stakeholders, working groups, or subject matter experts.

5.1.2.2 Portfolio Organizational Structure Analysis

Depending upon the size and complexity of an organization, a single person or a team may manage the portfolio, and senior management or a governing body may make decisions regarding portfolio components. The portfolio manager should assign performance review and reporting roles and responsibilities across each program, project, or operational component. Resources (information, human, and financial) are identified and made available to the portfolio components at the right time and returned to the enterprise once their purpose has been served.

5.1.2.3 Integration of Portfolio Management Plans

Portfolio management plan development is an iterative process. Subsidiary plans such as risk, communication, and performance management plans may be developed concurrently at the various stages of portfolio management. The subsidiary plans are considered as part of the portfolio management plan although they may be separate documents and contain references to the portfolio management plan. Integrating of subsidiary plans assumes the plans must be analyzed and aligned for consistency. If integration of subsidiary plans generates any changes in approved documents, those changes must be communicated to those responsible in order to resolve issues and reconcile changes.

5.1.3 Develop Portfolio Management Plan: Outputs

5.1.3.1 Portfolio Strategic Plan Updates

If the portfolio manager is unable to implement the portfolio, which was developed according to the current portfolio strategic plan, or if other developments warrant updates to portfolio strategy, the portfolio manager may recommend and gain approval to update the portfolio strategic plan.

5.1.3.2 Portfolio Management Plan

A portfolio management plan document is produced and approved. The portfolio management plan can include each of these sections:

- **Governance Model.** The governance model defines the way the organizational assets and resources are planned to be managed within the portfolio according to the specific environment of the organization. It establishes and tailors the decision-making rights and authorities, responsibilities, rules, and protocols needed to manage progress based on portfolio risk towards the achievement of their organizational strategy and objectives. This is accomplished through controls set up as gate reviews for each stage of a project. These gate reviews afford management the opportunity to review component progress and status at standard milestone dates throughout the lifecycle of the project. At each gate, management reviews the adjusted, forecasted value and updated risks to determine if the project should continue or if it should be put on hold or even cancelled. For purposes of this standard, organizational governance is the process by which an organization directs and controls its operations and strategic activities, and responds to the legitimate rights, expectations, and desires of its stakeholders. Portfolio governance is a set of interrelated organizational processes by which an organization selects and prioritizes components, and allocates limited internal resources to best accomplish organizational strategy and objectives.

  Roles and responsibilities should be clearly defined for specific roles such as portfolio manager, sponsors, portfolio stakeholders, executive stakeholders, and program and project managers. Roles and responsibilities need to be defined for portfolio management and for various governing bodies.

- **Portfolio Oversight.** A portfolio, program, or project management office (PMO) may support portfolio oversight by providing an effective way of sharing and optimizing scarce or common resources. Portfolio governance allocates resources at the required quantity and quality levels and at the time required. The PMO can also assist with communicating governance decisions, changes in the portfolio, and stakeholder communication according to sponsor and stakeholder requirements. If a PMO is to be utilized, the structure, responsibilities, and implementation approach will be documented in the portfolio management plan.

- **Managing Strategic Change.** The purpose of this process is to enable the portfolio manager to respond to changes in organizational strategy and objectives. Incremental, minor changes generally do not require changes to the portfolio. However, significant changes in the organization's environment often result in a new strategic direction, thereby impacting the portfolio resources and portfolio components, and rely on a defined change control structure. The portfolio management plan and portfolio governance processes should outline and manage the response to significant strategic change that impacts people, process, and assets or technology.

  A significant change in strategic direction will impact portfolio component categorization or prioritization, and this will require rebalancing the portfolio. Portfolio components may be terminated prior to delivery and new portfolio components approved and started in their place.

- **Change Control and Management.** Change control and management defines the process of managing changes to approved scope and requirements, schedules, and funding, including review and approval by stakeholders and governing bodies. This is to ensure that the outcome aligns to the organizational strategy, objectives meet targets and achieve return on investment, and resources are allocated appropriately. Change control may also include starting, stopping, and delaying portfolio components as resources are reprioritized to other portfolio components.

  Change management is performed through a change structure facilitating impact analysis (often provided in component proposals), deliberate review and approval or disapproval, prioritization, and scheduling of proposed change activities.

- **Balancing Portfolio and Managing Dependencies.** The plan documents the portfolio manager's method of portfolio balancing, which is the process of optimizing the mix of portfolio components to further the strategic objectives of the organization. Portfolio balancing supports the ability to plan and allocate resources according to strategic direction and the ability to maximize portfolio return within the organization's predefined desired risk profile (documented in the risk management plan).

- **Performance Management Planning.** This includes measuring and monitoring performance and value, portfolio performance reporting, and review. This section includes or refers to the portfolio performance management plan, which is described in Section 6.1.

- **Communication Planning.** This section includes or refers to the subsidiary portfolio communication management plan, which is described in Section 7.1.

- **Risk Management Planning.** This section includes or refers to the subsidiary portfolio risk management plan, which is described in Section 8.1.

- **Procurement Planning.** The plan should define any portfolio level procurement directives or standards that will be leveraged and which should be considered when managing the portfolio.

- **Managing Compliance.** Compliance with new legislation may require the postponement of active or planned portfolio components, thereby delaying or reducing the corresponding benefits. The plan will document how the portfolio manager will address compliance requirements.

- **Portfolio Prioritization Model.** The portfolio prioritization model is described in Section 4.1.2.3 and included in the portfolio strategic plan. A simple prioritization model such as a scorecard may be provided, containing criteria to ensure alignment to organizational strategy and objectives, expected return on investment (ROI), investment risk, and dependencies.

5.1.3.3 Portfolio Process Assets Updates

To manage the portfolio in alignment with the organizational strategy and the portfolio strategic plan, the portfolio manager may need to update various portfolio policies, processes, and guidelines as well as portfolio management knowledge bases. Portfolio process assets are described in Section 3.1.2.1.

5.2 Define Portfolio

The purpose of the Define Portfolio process is to create an up-to-date list of qualified portfolio components by identifying, categorizing, scoring, and ranking portfolio components. This process is required to produce an organized portfolio for ongoing evaluation, selection, and prioritization. This process ensures resources are or will be working on portfolio components that will provide the most significant value for the investment and are most strongly aligned to the organizational strategy and objectives. This process is closely aligned with the Optimize Portfolio process that optimizes the portfolio with the balanced portfolio component mix as described in Section 5.3.

Once identified, the list of existing and proposed portfolio components needs to be organized into relevant organization groups to which a common set of decision filters and criteria may be applied for evaluation, selection, and prioritization. The portfolio components in a given group have a common goal and are measured on the same basis regardless of their origin in the organization. The categorization of the portfolio components allows the organization to balance its investment and its risks between all strategic categories and goals.

All pertinent information is gathered and summarized for each portfolio component of the portfolio. The information may be qualitative and quantitative and comes from a variety of sources across the organization. The portfolio manager may revise the data several times until reaching the required level of completeness.

By its definition, portfolio management selects only portfolio components that align with the organizational strategy and meet defined criteria. Without a successful evaluation and definition process, unnecessary or poorly planned portfolio components may be incorporated within the portfolio and increase the workload of the organization, thus hampering the benefits realized from truly important and strategically aligned portfolio components.

Key activities within this process include:

- Identifying qualified portfolio components through the evaluation and assignment of key descriptors,
- Categorizing portfolio components to which a common set of decision filters and criteria may be applied, and
- Evaluating portfolio components with a ranking and scoring model comprising weighted key criteria.

Figure 5-4 shows the inputs, tools and techniques, and outputs. Figure 5-5 shows the data flow diagram.

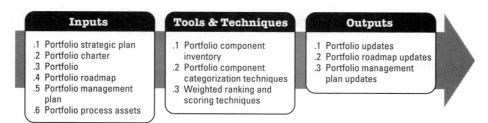

Figure 5-4. Define Portfolio: Inputs, Tools and Techniques, and Outputs

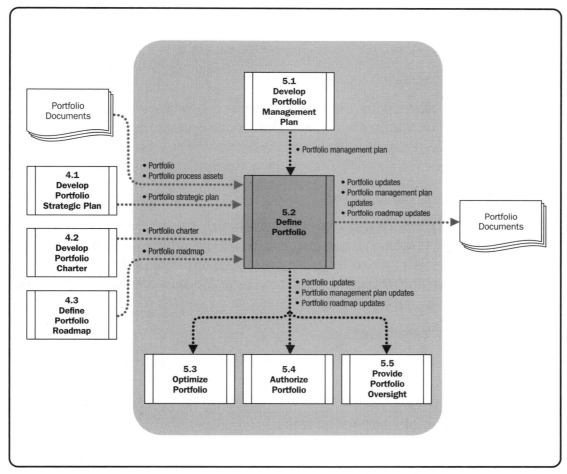

Figure 5-5. Define Portfolio: Data Flow Diagram

5.2.1   Define Portfolio: Inputs

5.2.1.1   Portfolio Strategic Plan

The portfolio strategic plan is described in Section 4.1. The portfolio strategic plan is used to align the portfolio with the organizational strategy and objectives. It contains the prioritization model and drives the need to define a portfolio and its individual portfolio components. To enable strategic alignment, preexisting portfolios or inventory of work shall be validated against strategy updates which could change the key descriptors, categorization, and organization of portfolio components. It may not be the sole source for determining which portfolio component to include but it is a key source to ensure an organization will meet its objectives.

5.2.1.2   Portfolio Charter

The portfolio charter, described in Section 4.2.3.2, is the document that formally authorizes the portfolio manager to apply portfolio resources to portfolio components within the portfolio. The charter is required by this process because it identifies the portfolio and subportfolios based on organizational areas in scope, hierarchies, and portfolio goals.

5.2.1.3   Portfolio

Regardless of whether a portfolio exists or if there is an inventory of work identified for inclusion in the portfolio, the portfolio components are the basis for defining or redefining the portfolio.

5.2.1.4   Portfolio Roadmap

The portfolio roadmap is necessary for this process because it summarizes strategic objectives, evolving aspects of the strategy by organizational areas, portfolio milestones, dependencies, challenges, and risks. The detailed identification, categorization, and ranking and scoring criteria may be derived from the portfolio roadmap. As a minimum, the defining criteria and categories should be in alignment with the portfolio roadmap.

5.2.1.5   Portfolio Management Plan

The portfolio management plan is created to describe the approach and intent of management in identifying, approving, procuring, prioritizing, balancing, managing, and reporting a portfolio of portfolio components. This process establishes the approach for defining, optimizing, and authorizing portfolio components. As an input to the Define Portfolio process, the portfolio management plan contains the guidance to evaluate portfolio components and make judgments to their alignment and priority.

5.2.1.6   Portfolio Process Assets

Portfolio process assets may include relevant templates, tools, data, and information regarding the portfolio and guidance for defining the portfolio components.

5.2.2   Define Portfolio: Tools and Techniques

Tools and techniques used to define the portfolio help the organization to produce a categorized list of portfolio components for ongoing evaluation and optimization.

The portfolio manager can apply a series of evaluation criteria associated with various organizational aspects. These criteria should be quantifiable so that they can be measured, ranked, and prioritized based on net benefit or value.

Some examples of evaluation criteria may include, but are not limited to:

- Organizational strategy alignment;
- Goals and objectives;
- Benefits, financial and nonfinancial;

- Market share, market growth, or new markets;
- Costs (lost opportunity costs);
- Dependencies, internal and external;
- Risks, internal and external;
- Legal/regulatory compliance;
- Human resources capabilities and capacities;
- Technology capabilities and capacities; and
- Urgency.

It is important to select evaluation criteria which best support the achievement of organizational strategy and objectives. Such criteria will also allow measuring the benefits contribution of a portfolio component.

5.2.2.1 Portfolio Component Inventory

The identification of qualified portfolio components determines whether or not a particular portfolio component qualifies to be part of the portfolio. The sponsor of a portfolio component uses a standard set of key descriptors when providing a proposal for a new portfolio component or a change to an existing portfolio component. The key descriptors ensure that all portfolio components are comparable. Descriptors and criteria may be used for filtering or eliminating new portfolio components by having associated acceptance levels.

A preliminary comparison of all inventoried portfolio components against the portfolio component definition is used to identify portfolio components that meet requirements for consideration. The portfolio component definition is used to make a first screening on the portfolio component list. For example, to be part of the portfolio, a portfolio component should be greater than a predetermined minimum size and be in line with the basic strategic goals.

Each descriptor is defined and the corresponding evaluation criteria are predetermined. Key descriptors may include, but are not limited to:

- Portfolio component number,
- Portfolio component code,
- Portfolio component description,
- Type of portfolio component,
- Strategic goals supported,
- Quantitative benefits,
- Qualitative benefits,
- Portfolio component customer,
- Portfolio component sponsor,
- Key stakeholders, and
- Resources required.

5.2.2.2   Portfolio Component Categorization Techniques

Assigning portfolio components to predetermined categories helps to compare portfolio components that address similar organizational needs and strategic concerns. It also facilitates portfolio optimization by ensuring that portfolio components are selected and managed within a set of categories addressing the organizational strategy and objectives.

Each identified portfolio component, along with the key descriptors, is compared to the categorization criteria and is assigned to a given category for the purpose of scoring, ranking, evaluating, and selecting between similar portfolio components.

The number of categories is usually limited. Examples include:

- Increased profitability (revenue increase, generation, cost reduction and avoidance),
- Risk reduction,
- Efficiency improvement,
- Regulatory/compliance,
- Market share increase,
- Process improvement,
- Continuous improvement,
- Foundational (e.g., investments that build the infrastructure to grow the business), and
- Business imperatives (e.g., internal toolkit, IT compatibility, or upgrades).

5.2.2.3   Weighted Ranking and Scoring Techniques

Weighted ranking and scoring techniques are used for ranking and scoring portfolio components within each category based on values assigned. Portfolio components are ranked according to preestablished criteria as illustrated in Figures 5-6 and 5-7.

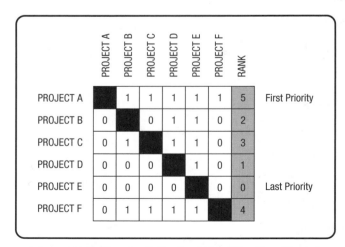

Figure 5-6. Single-Criterion Prioritization Model

The single-criterion approach, as illustrated in Figure 5-6, is a pair-wise comparison of different portfolio components with one another, to rank them hierarchically from the one that should be given the highest priority to the one that should be the least priority within a given portfolio. Using a single criterion like priority of each project to all of the other projects and assigning a value of 1 if judged superior, the highest score becomes the highest ranking.

In the second example using multiple criteria, the projects are ranked based on the criteria to assign the highest priority to the project with the lowest score (as shown in Figure 5-7).

PROJECTS	Criterion 1		Criterion 2 * Probability of Success		Criterion 3		Criterion 4		PRIORITY	
	Measure	Rank	Result	Rank	Level of Importance	Rank	Measure	Rank	Score	Priority
Project 1	16.0	2	8.8 ($11M X 80%)	2	5 (++)	1	$2M	1	1.50	1
Project 3	14.0	4	18.9 ($21M X 90%)	1	4	2	$2.5M	2	2.25	2
Project 4	15.5	3	8.45 ($13M X 65%)	3	2	4	$3M	3	3.25	3
Project 2	19.0	1	5.95 ($7M X 85%)	4	1 (--)	6	$4.3M	4	3.75	4
Project 5	10.0	6	5.4 ($6M X 90%)	5	3	3	$5.2M	6	5.00	5
Project 6	12.0	5	2.1 ($3M X 70%)	6	1.5	5	$4.6M	5	5.25	6

Figure 5-7. Multiple-Criteria Weighted Ranking

Scoring models provide another possible method used to evaluate portfolio components and make them comparable. A scoring model consists of a series of evaluation criteria having a weight expressed as a percentage and a score. The weight for each criterion is expressed in percentages (the total needs to add up to 100%) and determines the relative importance of each criterion in the portfolio component evaluation. The score applies to each criterion and should be discriminating (such as 0, 5, and 10). The score measures whether or not each criterion is met. Each scoring level needs to be clearly defined to ensure consistent evaluation from portfolio component to portfolio component. The score multiplied by the weight provides a value for each criterion and the total of all of these criteria values is the total value of the portfolio component (as shown in Figure 5-8).

SCORING MODEL		Evaluation					
List of Criteria	Weight	Low	Medium	High	Score	Total	
Criteria 1	20%	0	5	10	10	2	
Criteria 2	20%	0	5	10	10	2	Indicator "Y"
Criteria 3	10%	0	5	10	5	0.5	
Criteria 4	15%	0	5	10	10	1.5	
Criteria 5	5%	0	5	10	5	0.25	
Criteria 6	5%	0	5	10	0	0	
Criteria 7	5%	0	5	10	10	0.5	
Criteria 8	5%	0	5	10	5	0.25	Indicator "X"
Criteria 9	10%	0	5	10	0	0	
Criteria 10	5%	0	5	10	5	0.25	
TOTAL WEIGHT = 100%				TOTAL SCORE		7.25	
				Indicator "Y" (0 to 1)		0.83	
				Indicator "X" (0 to 1)		0.4	

Figure 5-8. Multi-Criteria Scoring Model

Mandatory criteria, such as regulatory or operational requirements, deserve particular attention. Portfolio components that are required to comply with such mandates need to be noted to ensure their inclusion in the final portfolio regardless of their scoring and ranking.

5.2.3 Define Portfolio: Outputs

5.2.3.1 Portfolio Updates

The portfolio is updated with portfolio components that have been strategically aligned, evaluated, and prioritized for ongoing selection, authorization, and optimization. A list of identified and ranked portfolio components is produced for each category. Portfolio components may be compared by category or for the entire portfolio. The portfolio component key descriptors are used for categorizing, evaluating, and selecting portfolio components in the portfolio. The key descriptors also provide context for monitoring and optimizing portfolio component performance to ensure benefits delivery.

5.2.3.2 Portfolio Roadmap Updates

The portfolio roadmap may require updating when the result of the Define Portfolio process requires a change in the portfolio components included or excluded or in the dependencies in the roadmap.

5.2.3.3 Portfolio Management Plan Updates

The portfolio management plan may require updating when the result of the Define Portfolio process indicates a change in the portfolio management approach is required, such as a change in the prioritization criteria. Other examples are when the categories or classification of portfolio components are revised or the approach is changed on how a portfolio is optimized, authorized, and monitored.

5.3 Optimize Portfolio

The purpose of this process is to optimize and balance the portfolio for performance and value delivery. Portfolio optimization involves evaluating the portfolio based on the organization's selection criteria, ranking those portfolio components, and creating the portfolio component mix with the greatest potential to collectively support the organizational strategy. Portfolio optimization includes planning and allocating resources according to organizational strategy and objectives and maximizing portfolio return within the organization's predefined risk profile and tolerances. It is important to balance the portfolio with respect to the diverse goals of the organization, such as financial, organizational development and operational performance goals. This process is closely aligned with the Define Portfolio process described in Section 5.2.

Portfolio optimization evaluates trade-offs of portfolio objectives, such as the management of risk and return, balancing short-term goals against long-term goals, and balancing project types to align with the organizational strategy and objectives. Limited resources are also balanced across the portfolio to reflect strategic priorities. Portfolio components that deliver a lower level of benefit are removed from the portfolio to allow the organization to focus its resources on higher priority portfolio components that deliver more value. Optimization also incorporates groupings of portfolio components to ensure that portfolio components include all component dependencies, including cost and benefit dependencies for the entire group.

Balancing activities involves reviewing selected and prioritized portfolio components. The portfolio is then balanced to support organizational strategy and objectives using predefined portfolio management criteria, the organization's desired risk profile, portfolio performance metrics, and capacity constraints. Maintaining the portfolio "as is" or adjusting the portfolio is made at completion of the optimization activities.

Portfolio components can be balanced with one another, usually within the same category (categorization also being an attempt to balance portfolio components to address all of the diverse concerns and organizational strategy), using a variety of qualitative and quantitative methods and tools to support the decision-making process and to allocate a budget.

Key activities within this process include:

- Assigning or reassigning, scoring, or weighting criteria for ranking portfolio components;

- Performing risk analysis on portfolio components based on the organization's risk profile;

- Evaluating and determining performance and expected value and benefits (financial and non-financial) of portfolio components;

- Determining resource (human, assets, and technology) capability, resource capacity available, and constraints for portfolio components;

- Determining which portfolio components should receive the highest priority within the portfolio; and

- Identifying portfolio components to be suspended, reprioritized, or terminated based on the balancing or rebalancing activities.

Figure 5-9 shows the inputs, tools and techniques, and outputs. Figure 5-10 shows the data flow diagram.

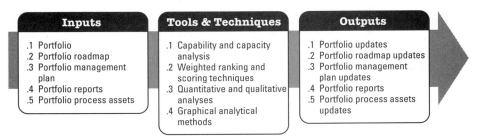

Figure 5-9. Optimize Portfolio: Inputs, Tools and Techniques, and Outputs

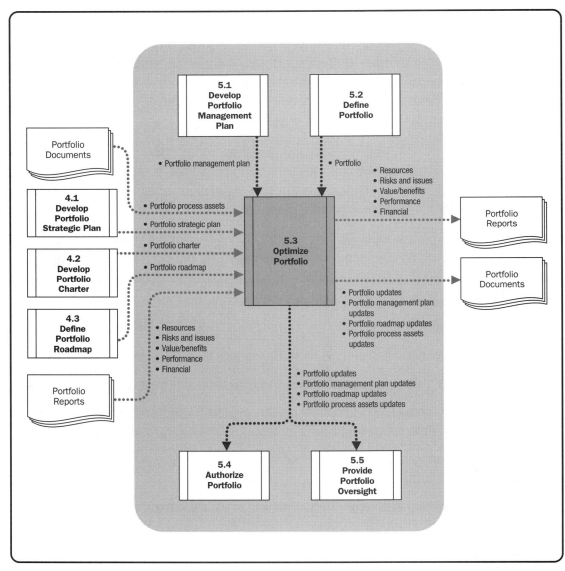

Figure 5-10. Optimize Portfolio: Data Flow Diagram

5.3.1 Optimize Portfolio: Inputs

5.3.1.1 Portfolio

The portfolio's current active and inactive portfolio components are evaluated for optimization to ensure that resources are allocated to achieve organizational strategy and objectives that deliver the most value to the organization.

5.3.1.2 Portfolio Roadmap

The portfolio roadmap provides the organizational strategy "to-be" vision for the portfolio that will guide the portfolio optimization, including the dependencies, timing, and sequencing of portfolio components. The portfolio roadmap is described in Section 4.3.3.1.

5.3.1.3 Portfolio Management Plan

The portfolio management plan, described in Section 5.1.3.2, provides the Optimize Portfolio process with the approach for defining, optimizing, and authorizing portfolio components. The plan documents the intended approach to managing the portfolio, subportfolios, and portfolio components in order to meet the organizational strategy.

5.3.1.4 Portfolio Reports

Various portfolio reports are reviewed and analyzed to optimize the portfolio. Portfolio risk reports are used to understand major risks associated with existing portfolio components and any potential issues which may arise from implementing the portfolio. Resource pool report data are reviewed to understand resource allocation, availability, and capability. Portfolio capability and capacity reports provide the maximum capability of the organization to meet resource demand or requirements. Additional portfolio reports that assist in portfolio optimization are performance, financial, and value or benefits.

5.3.1.5 Portfolio Process Assets

Portfolio process assets, described in Section 3.1.2.1, may contain relevant data, tools, templates, and information regarding the portfolio and guidance on optimizing the portfolio.

5.3.2 Optimize Portfolio: Tools and Techniques

The organization can use tools and techniques to create a list of portfolio components that will be considered for prioritization. This may include using the results of the scoring model to eliminate those portfolio components not meeting acceptance threshold scores with respect to one or several predetermined criteria and indicators. Although this process focuses on the value of individual portfolio components, the capacity analyses will also constrain the portfolio components to organizational capacity constraints.

Tools and techniques for the Optimize Portfolio process are designed to assist portfolio managers and governing bodies in their prioritization of portfolio components. The criteria may be the same as used in the scoring model to evaluate and select portfolio components. For prioritization, the portfolio components will be compared to separate and combined entities in an effort to prioritize them in a coherent way to ensure optimal alignment with the organizational strategy. Tools and techniques also help the organization to effectively select and implement a portfolio with the best overall alignment with the organizational strategy.

5.3.2.1 Capability and Capacity Analysis

Exceeding the available resource capacity jeopardizes the portfolio's ability to attain its goals and benefits. Protecting resource capacity directly supports portfolio component execution by ensuring that resources are available to accomplish portfolio objectives. Capacity management is a critical component of portfolio optimization as it enables the organization to achieve maximum portfolio benefits given current resource constraints. The organizational capacity analyses comprise the following three analyses:

- **Human resource capability and capacity analysis.** The human resource capability and capacity analysis is performed to understand the capabilities and capacity of the organization to source and execute the selected portfolio components, and to determine the constraint generated by capability, such as certain skill-set limitations. Internal resource capacity needs to be measured and external resource availability needs to be established in order to have a complete picture. The human resource capability and capacity will be limiting factors for the number of portfolio components the organization can execute.

- **Financial capability and capacity analysis.** The financial capability and capacity analysis is performed to understand the capability and capacity of the organization to finance the selected portfolio components. Internal financial capacity needs to be measured and external financial resource availability (capability) needs to be established in order to have a complete picture. The financial resource capability and capacity will be constraining factors for the number of portfolio components or the size of portfolio components the organization can execute.

- **Asset capacity and capability analysis.** The asset capacity and capability analysis is performed to understand the physical needs, by determining the type of assets (equipment, buildings, systems, etc.), of the organization available to support the selected portfolio components and to understand the constraints generated by certain asset limitations. The asset capacity will be a limiting factor for the number of portfolio components and the size of portfolio components the organization can execute.

5.3.2.2 Weighted Ranking and Scoring Techniques

These are the techniques of weighting and ranking portfolio components within each category based on values assigned. Portfolio components are ranked according to preestablished criteria as illustrated in Section 5.2.2.3 as the single-criterion prioritization model and multiple-criteria weighted ranking, and multi-criteria scoring model.

5.3.2.3 Quantitative and Qualitative Analyses

Quantitative and qualitative analyses include various analyses that help in optimizing the portfolio. These analyses include:

- **Cost-Benefit Analysis.** This analysis may be performed with any financial analytical method preferred by the organization. These methods may include: net present value (NPV), discounted cash flow (DCF), internal rate of return (IRR), cost benefit ratio, payback, and options analysis.

- **Quantitative Analysis.** Quantitative analysis may include the use of spreadsheets or other tools to examine factors of interest, such as resource loading requirements over time or cash flow.

- **Scenario Analysis.** This analytical method enables decision makers to create a variety of portfolio scenarios using different combinations of both potential portfolio components and current portfolio components and evaluating their possible outcomes based on various assumptions. The analysis can be further enhanced by incorporating numerous baselines.

- **Probability Analysis.** These methods may include decision trees, flowcharts, and Monte Carlo simulation. Portfolio components are evaluated using success and failure probabilities and ranges of impacts if they occur for estimated cost, time, anticipated revenues, risk, and other criteria.

- **SWOT Analysis.** Market and competitor analysis includes determining the value of portfolio components in the market place and how portfolio components may affect (or be affected by) competitors. A SWOT (strengths, weaknesses, opportunities, and threats) analysis can be used to ensure market and competitor information is comprehensively and holistically considered.

- **Market/Competitor Analysis.** Market and competitor analysis includes determining the value of portfolio components in the market place and how portfolio components may affect or be affected by competitors.

- **Business Value Analysis.** Predetermining the values to improve the market value or organizational improvement and then applying those values to the portfolio components is another technique. In this context, the data may be qualitative or quantitative and as long as the sponsor agrees with the order of execution, the value is correct.

5.3.2.4 Graphical Analytical Methods

These are graphical methods such as risk vs. return charts, histograms, pie charts, and other methods to visualize the portfolio. Figures 5-11 and 5-12 are two of the graphical representations often used by organizations to balance and monitor their portfolios.

Figure 5-11 presents a typical bubble graph that helps compare and balance portfolio components according to some preestablished portfolio component balancing criteria. Each bubble is a portfolio component, and the size of the bubble represents an additional variable, such as cost or net present value. Color may mean yet another criteria or categorization.

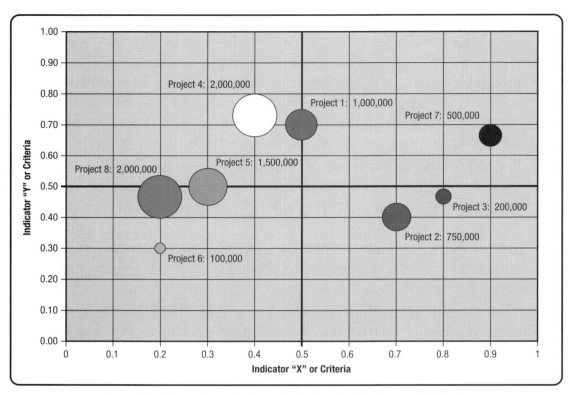

Figure 5-11. Portfolio Balancing Using Indicators or Criteria

Figure 5-12 illustrates another variant of the bubble graph, displaying portfolio components according to the category they belong to and the organizational unit impacted/targeted by the portfolio component. The bubble graph also uses other indicators from the scoring model or new indicators concerned with portfolio balance where each bubble is a portfolio component and the size of the bubble represents an additional variable, such as cost or net present value. The color of a bubble might refer to a specific qualitative criteria required to measure balance.

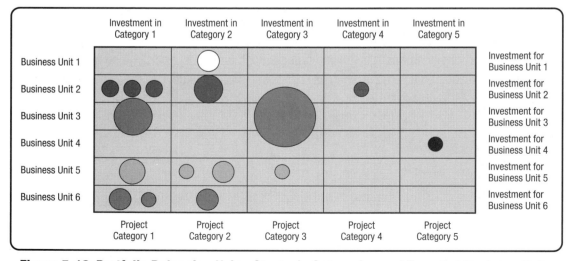

Figure 5-12. Portfolio Balancing Using Strategic Categories and Targeted Business Units

5.3.3 Optimize Portfolio: Outputs

5.3.3.1 Portfolio Updates

Portfolio optimization is performed on a recurring basis, and the portfolio is updated, including portfolio component relationships, ranking criteria, priorities, dependencies, goals and other portfolio component information that are updated as a result of portfolio optimization. The rationale for the decision to remove a portfolio component from the portfolio or include a portfolio component in the portfolio is added to the portfolio component information.

Portfolio component budget and resource approvals or exceptions should be updated on the portfolio list. This is an iterative process that takes into account both internal and external factors that change the costs, risks, or values of the portfolio components.

5.3.3.2 Portfolio Roadmap Updates

Portfolio roadmap is updated as the portfolio is optimized. The organizational areas, portfolio components, and high-level timeline may be changed due to optimization.

5.3.3.3 Portfolio Management Plan Updates

As a result of the Optimize Portfolio process, the optimizing approach, criteria, and other information about maintaining a balanced portfolio may need to be updated in the portfolio management plan.

5.3.3.4 Portfolio Reports

Various portfolio reports may be updated as a result of the portfolio optimization process, such as resources, risks/issues, value/benefits, performance, and financials. During the portfolio optimization process, as existing portfolio components or newly selected portfolio components are evaluated, risks ratings and types of response may be created or changed in risk reports. Reports about resources, such as capability and capacity, may also be updated due to optimization.

5.3.3.5 Portfolio Process Asset Updates

Portfolio process asset updates may be needed after the portfolio is optimized. The process assets include formal and informal plans, policies, procedures, and guidelines. The optimize portfolio procedures and guidelines information may need to be updated and stored.

5.4 Authorize Portfolio

The purpose of this process is to activate selected portfolio components by allocating resources to develop component proposals or execute portfolio components; update relevant portfolio reports such as funding updates, resource assignments, and allocations; and document governance decisions. The changes in the portfolio and related decisions are communicated to interested parties, governing bodies, stakeholders, and portfolio, program, and project managers. Key activities within the process include:

- Authorizing portfolio component proposal development or portfolio component execution;
- Allocating resources to authorized portfolio components;

- Reallocating funding and resources from deactivated and terminated portfolio components to activated portfolio components or the resource pools; and
- Communicating changes and decisions for the authorized portfolio components.

Figure 5-13 shows the inputs, tools and techniques, and outputs for this process. Figure 5-14 shows the data flow diagram.

Inputs	Tools & Techniques	Outputs
.1 Portfolio .2 Portfolio management plan .3 Portfolio reports	.1 Portfolio authorization process .2 Portfolio management information system	.1 Portfolio updates .2 Portfolio management plan updates .3 Portfolio reports .4 Portfolio process assets updates

Figure 5-13. Authorize Portfolio: Inputs, Tools and Techniques, and Outputs

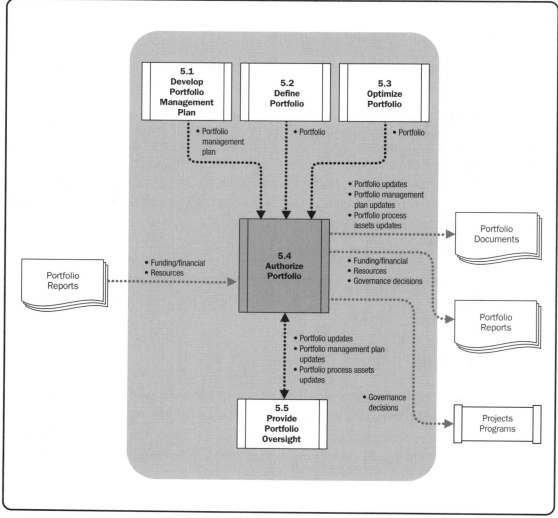

Figure 5-14. Authorize Portfolio: Data Flow Diagram

5.4.1 Authorize Portfolio: Inputs

5.4.1.1 Portfolio

The portfolio includes a list of portfolio components and related descriptive information, which have been approved in previous processes and need to be authorized with their respective funding and resource requirements. The portfolio contains a list of portfolio components for deactivation with remaining funding and resources that need to be returned to the organization's funding and resource pools.

5.4.1.2 Portfolio Management Plan

The portfolio management plan, described in Section 5.1.3.2, describes the process to authorize the portfolio components to allocate and reallocate resources and funding and to define the key communication needs associated with the portfolio management process, focusing on the proactive and targeted development and delivery of key messages to the key stakeholders.

5.4.1.3 Portfolio Reports

Various portfolio reports are reviewed and analyzed to authorize portfolio components. The primary types of reports for this process are financials/funding, resources, and governance decisions. For example, the portfolio budget (annual or in multi-year format) is the funding that the organization is allocating to the portfolio for executing portfolio components and for meeting organizational strategy and objectives. In the authorization process, the portfolio funding is divided between the different portfolio components according to the contractual milestones of each of the portfolio components.

The resource reports include human resources (such as project managers, subject matter experts, solution architects, etc.), physical/major shared assets (such as IT and telecommunication or specialized equipment, laboratories and installations), and financial resources. The resource reports will be used to allocate resources to the authorized portfolio components. The central management of resources maximizes the efficiency of resource use and aligns to the overall portfolio goals and objectives and ensures the right resources are available on time.

Governance decision reports authorize components and provide detailed information on the authorization justification.

5.4.2 Authorize Portfolio: Tools and Techniques

5.4.2.1 Portfolio Authorization Technique

The authorization tools and techniques specify the activities to formally authorize a new portfolio or portfolio components, to effect funding allocations and transfers, and to report and communicate the results.

5.4.2.2 Portfolio Management Information System

The portfolio management information system is a tool used to execute the Authorize Portfolio process by indicating which portfolio components have been assigned resources. All changes and updates made to the authorized portfolio components are communicated by means of the updated portfolio management information system and other communication methods.

5.4.3 Authorize Portfolio: Outputs

5.4.3.1 Portfolio Updates

The portfolio is updated with the status of newly authorized portfolio components, their respective funding and allocated resources, and any other related information that is applicable. Portfolio components authorization is documented to formally begin work on authorized portfolio components. The communication should include stakeholders and other portfolio component support functions.

5.4.3.2 Portfolio Management Plan Updates

The portfolio management plan and its subsidiary plans may need to be updated for various reasons related to the Authorize Portfolio process. An example may be updates for budget/funding or resource allocation or updates to the process for evaluating portfolio component authorization if the current established process does not meet the portfolio management requirements.

5.4.3.3 Portfolio Reports

Various portfolio reports may be updated as a result of the Authorize Portfolio process, such as resources, assets (financials and nonfinancial), and governance decisions. During the Authorize Portfolio process, as portfolio components are authorized, there are changes in the funding and resource pools. Other reports may be updated due to the authorization activities and results.

For example, the portfolio funding (annual or multiyear budgets) is updated to reflect the funding allocated to the authorized portfolio components in the portfolio, and the funding, which is reallocated from terminated or cancelled portfolio components and ready for use in funding new approved portfolio components or funds, is transferred to the funding pool. Another example is a report that shows the updated resource pool reflecting the resources allocated to the authorized portfolio components in the portfolio and the resources reallocated from terminated or cancelled portfolio components.

5.4.3.4 Portfolio Process Asset Updates

Portfolio process asset updates may be needed after Authorize Portfolio is implemented. The process assets include tools and templates, formal and informal plans, policies, procedures, and guidelines. The Authorize Portfolio component procedures and guidelines information may need to be updated. Examples of updates are human resource assignment procedures or transferring funding among components to and from the funding pool.

5.5 Provide Portfolio Oversight

The purpose of the Provide Portfolio Oversight process is to monitor the portfolio to ensure alignment with organizational strategy and objectives and make governance decisions in response to:

- Portfolio performance;
- Portfolio component proposals and changes;
- Availability of resource (human, technology, and other assets) capability and capacity;

- Funding allocations and future investment requirements; and
- Risks and issues.

Key activities within this process include:

- Reviewing information on portfolio resources, risks, performance, and financial information;
- Conducting recurring and nonrecurring governance meetings for reviews and decision making;
- Ensuring compliance with organizational standards;
- Reporting portfolio changes and information on resources, risks, performance, and financials; and
- Communicating governance decisions.

Figure 5-15 shows the inputs, tools and techniques, and outputs. Figure 5-16 shows the data flow diagram.

Figure 5-15. Provide Portfolio Oversight: Inputs, Tools and Techniques, and Outputs

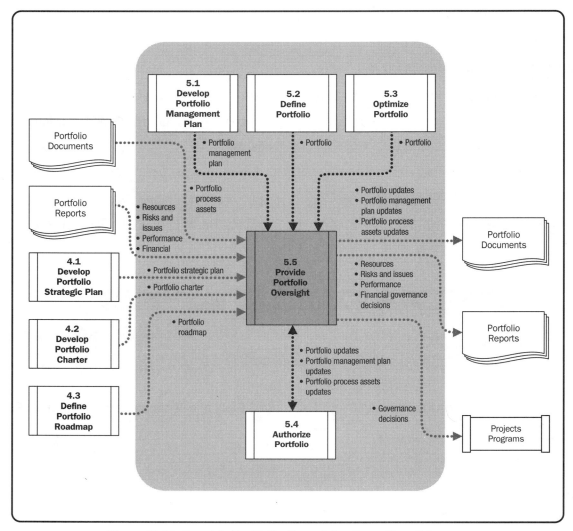

Figure 5-16. Provide Portfolio Oversight: Data Flow Diagram

5.5.1 Provide Portfolio Oversight: Inputs

5.5.1.1   Portfolio

The portfolio provides critical information on portfolio components that is required by portfolio oversight in order to consider portfolio component proposals and changes and funding allocations. Portfolio oversight is concerned with making sure that the portfolio's current portfolio components and planned or future initiatives will address organizational strategy and objectives.

5.5.1.2   Portfolio Roadmap

The portfolio roadmap, which is organized in a chronological fashion, provides high-level strategic direction and dependencies within the portfolio to allow for oversight. The portfolio roadmap provides an integrated view of the portfolio strategy and is a useful tool for portfolio communication. The roadmap also shows the timeline of the portfolio components as these may change over time.

5.5.1.3 Portfolio Management Plan

The portfolio management plan provides portfolio oversight with the portfolio management approach and establishes how a portfolio is defined, organized, optimized, and controlled. The portfolio management plan documents the intended approach for managing the portfolio and its portfolio components in order to meet the organizational strategy.

5.5.1.4 Portfolio Reports

Portfolio reports, such as portfolio performance, resource capability and capacity, risks/issues, and financial information, may be reviewed by portfolio oversight to evaluate the portfolio and its individual components to decide what actions should be taken in order to minimize risk and maximize the benefits that the portfolio delivers to the organization.

Portfolio reports assist in determining whether the portfolio is performing as expected and to evaluate whether the portfolio benefits align with organizational strategy. Portfolio reports are described in Sections 6.2.3.1 and 6.3.1.4.

5.5.1.5 Portfolio Process Assets

The Provide Portfolio Oversight process may utilize portfolio process assets when reviewing, optimizing, authorizing, and controlling the portfolio. Portfolio process assets include portfolio policies, processes and procedures, and portfolio knowledge bases. These process assets may include historical performance information, governance decisions, and open issues. Portfolio process assets are described in Section 3.1.2.1.

5.5.2 Provide Portfolio Oversight: Tools and Techniques

5.5.2.1 Portfolio Review Meetings

Portfolio review meetings are held by the portfolio governing body in order to review the current status of the portfolio and to determine if any decisions need to be made regarding the portfolio and its portfolio components. These meetings are typically recurring, formal in nature, scheduled around significant portfolio milestones, or triggered by external events such as financial drivers, regulatory changes, and completion of significant portfolio components or deliverables.

5.5.2.2 Elicitation Techniques

There are numerous elicitation techniques that can be used when providing portfolio oversight and gathering potential issues and risks. Examples of elicitation techniques are compiling status reporting, facilitating meetings, and conducting questionnaires and surveys. Elicitation techniques are described in Section 5.1.2.1.

5.5.3 Provide Portfolio Oversight: Outputs

5.5.3.1 Portfolio Updates

The portfolio is updated as a result of decisions made by the portfolio governing body during their formal or informal portfolio governance meetings. For example, when the governing body decides that a portfolio component needs to be added, terminated, or changed in some fashion, the portfolio is updated. Once the governing body makes a decision that changes the current portfolio in some way, the decision is communicated to stakeholders, governing bodies, and portfolio component managers. The method for documenting and communicating the governance decisions may be a spreadsheet, a text document, or found within the portfolio management information.

5.5.3.2 Portfolio Management Plan Updates

The portfolio management plan and its collection of subsidiary plans may be revised as the result of a governing body decision regarding the portfolio oversight approach, decision tracking, or other types of status reporting.

5.5.3.3 Portfolio Reports

Portfolio reports such as portfolio performance, resource capability and capacity, risks/issues, and financial information may be updated during the Provide Portfolio Oversight process based on determined risks/issues, actions, and decisions made to change the portfolio or to maximize the benefits that the portfolio delivers to the organization.

5.5.3.4 Portfolio Process Assets Updates

During the activities of the Provide Portfolio Oversight process, it may be determined that portfolio process assets require updating, such as portfolio policies, processes and procedures, and portfolio knowledge bases. These updates may also include governance decisions and open issues.

PORTFOLIO PERFORMANCE MANAGEMENT

The objective of portfolio management is to determine the optimal mix and sequencing of proposed projects to best achieve the organizational strategy and objectives. Portfolio performance management is the systematic planning, measurement, and monitoring of the portfolio's organizational value through achievement against these strategic goals (business value is explained in Section 1). In addition, the performance management process manages the sourcing of key resources such as finance, assets, and human resources to ensure optimal returns.

Organizational strategy can be expressed through the organization's vision and mission, including orientation to markets, competition, and other environmental factors. Effective organizational strategy provides defined directions for development and growth in addition to performance measurement metrics for success. Portfolio performance management is critical in closing the gap between organizational strategy and the fulfillment of that strategy. Organizations can further facilitate the alignment of these components by strengthening organizational enablers such as structural, cultural, technological, and human resource practices.

Through the identification of organization value areas where components are most likely to impact, the organization can clearly justify why and how investing resources in the selected projects will benefit the organization. Sometimes a project may affect two or three value areas simultaneously, such as increasing revenues, bringing in new customers, and increasing revenue from existing customers. Acceptance that not every project will be valuable to the organization is the key to making decisions.

Performance metrics are the mechanism used for targeting areas of measurement for assessing how the mix of portfolio components is performing. Quantitative and qualitative, in addition to tangible and intangible, measures are used.

Examples of the quantitative measures include:

- Increases in revenue attributable to the portfolio,
- Decreases in cost attributable to the portfolio,
- Change in net present value (NPV) of the portfolio,
- Return on investment (ROI) of the portfolio,
- Internal rate of return (IRR) of the portfolio, and
- Percentage by which cycle times are reduced due to the portfolio.

Examples of the intangible, qualitative measures include:

- Degree of strategic alignment,
- Degree to which portfolio and organizational risks have been adequately managed by undertaking the portfolio components,

- Recognition of legal and regulatory compliance, and
- Sustainability and corporate responsibility.

Typical attributes of projects that are collected and analyzed in a portfolio include each project's total expected cost, consumption of scarce resources (human, financial, or material), expected timeline and schedule of investment, magnitude and timing of benefits to be realized, and the relationship or interdependencies with other components in the portfolio. Portfolio value is delivered when the portfolio components are utilized by the organization, community, customer, or other portfolio beneficiaries. Benefits are sometimes not realized until long after the end of active work on a portfolio component.

Many organizations will express progress in the form of a dashboard, which can quickly communicate status to the sponsor and stakeholders on how the portfolio is performing against expectations. In addition, reporting is communicated through variance reports, benefits realization, and resource utilization reports.

The Portfolio Performance Management processes are (see Figure 6-1 for overview):

6.1 Develop Portfolio Performance Management Plan—Developing the performance management plan as to how portfolio value is defined and realized through the portfolio measurements and targets, alignment to organizational strategy and objectives, and roles and responsibilities in executing the plan.

6.2 Manage Supply and Demand—Identifying and allocating the required portfolio resources capacity and capabilities according to each component proposal or plan.

6.3 Manage Portfolio Value—Measuring, capturing, validating, and reporting portfolio value at an aggregate level delivered by portfolio components with the goal of maximizing return on investment (within an acceptable level of risk).

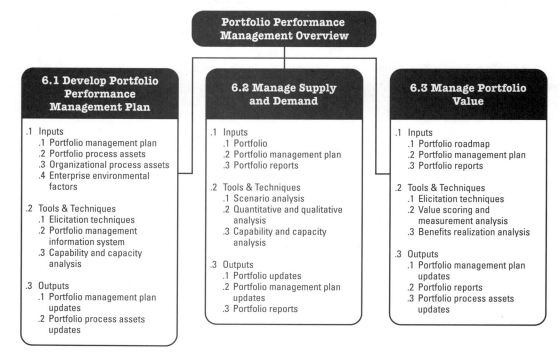

Figure 6-1. Portfolio Performance Management Overview

Figure 6-1 provides an overview of the processes and their respective inputs, tools and techniques, and outputs for this Knowledge Area.

6.1 Develop Portfolio Performance Management Plan

The portfolio performance management plan is a subsidiary plan of the portfolio management plan or a component of the portfolio management plan. It explains how portfolio value is defined and details how portfolio components are allocated for financial, human, and material or equipment resources. Performance planning starts with reviewing the portfolio goals set in the portfolio strategic plan, and the objectives set to reach these goals. Performance management is a discipline for measuring and analyzing progress against goals to determine if changes to the objectives, strategies, metrics, or to the portfolio component mix need to be made. Recommendations for changes are based on performance, changes in resource capability or capacity (constraints), benefits realization, assumptions, dependencies, or risks.

Portfolio resource management planning determines how resource capacity will be managed against resource utilization and changing demand to ensure a portfolio component mix generates maximum value. The performance management plan also defines the parameters and sets acceptable ranges for optimal resource capacity utilization such as insourcing versus outsourcing levels, funding levels based on financial leverage, and risk exposure policies.

Portfolio value planning covers how the realization of benefits associated with the portfolio components are tracked and optimized for maximum organization value. Organization value is more than just economic value, in that it includes revenue growth and increased operating margins. It also includes other forms of value, such as employee or customer satisfaction, contribution to the community, enhancement or protection of reputation, and branding, integrity of the organization's products or services, or protection of environmental resources.

Portfolio reporting will focus on providing stakeholders and the governing body with metrics to determine whether the portfolio is meeting the organizational strategy and objectives. It should enable the portfolio sponsors to quickly understand the status of the portfolio's progress in achieving the expected benefits.

To a lesser degree, portfolio reporting will also provide those responsible for executing portfolio components with meaningful information on the status of the respective portfolio components in the context of other components and the overall portfolio. This level of portfolio reporting is important to optimize resource utilization against organizational priorities.

The performance management plan documents how the organization plans to measure, monitor, control and report (1) portfolio performance, (2) resource management, and (3) portfolio value.

Figure 6-2 shows the inputs, tools and techniques, and outputs. Figure 6-3 shows the data flow diagram.

Inputs	Tools & Techniques	Outputs
.1 Portfolio management plan .2 Portfolio process assets .3 Organizational process assets .4 Enterprise environmental factors	.1 Elicitation techniques .2 Portfolio management information system .3 Capability and capacity analysis	.1 Portfolio management plan updates .2 Portfolio process assets updates

Figure 6-2. Develop Portfolio Performance Management Plan: Inputs, Tools and Techniques, and Outputs

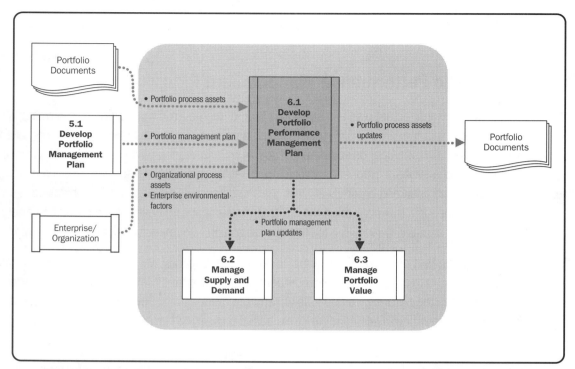

Figure 6-3. Develop Portfolio Performance Management Plan: Data Flow Diagram

6.1.1   Develop Portfolio Performance Management Plan: Inputs

6.1.1.1   Portfolio Management Plan

The portfolio performance management plan is a subsidiary plan or component of the portfolio management plan. When planning for portfolio performance, the portfolio management plan provides stakeholder expectations and requirements, governance model, strategic change framework, planning, procurement, and oversight processes including direction for performance, communication, and risk management. This information is critical when building a framework for managing resources and generating value.

6.1.1.2   Portfolio Process Assets

Several portfolio process assets are helpful in developing a performance management plan. These are various portfolio-related documents such as the portfolio strategic plan, portfolio charter, processes, policies, procedures, and knowledge bases used by the portfolio management office and stakeholders. These may also include various schedules such as the resource schedule, funding schedule, resource work calendar, benefits schedule, and portfolio component schedule. Portfolio process assets are described in Section 3.

6.1.1.3   Organizational Process Assets

Organizational process assets include plans, processes, policies, procedures and knowledge bases, specific to and used by the performing organization. These assets, although external to the portfolio, may provide direction to develop the portfolio performance management plan. One example is human-resource-related policies. Organizational process assets are described in Section 3.

6.1.1.4 Enterprise Environmental Factors

Enterprise environmental factors (EEF) are internal or external conditions, which are not under the control of the portfolio organization, that influence, constrain, or direct portfolio performance. EEFs may have a positive or negative influence on the portfolio. Those EEFs impacting the portfolio performance management plan may include organizational culture, structure, and human resources. Enterprise environmental factors are described in Section 3.

6.1.2 Develop Portfolio Performance Management Plan: Tools and Techniques

6.1.2.1 Elicitation Techniques

Planning techniques, such as elicitation, are foundational to the performance management plan development. In elicitation, stakeholders and key subject matter experts are consulted during planning meetings, brainstorming sessions, interviews, or surveys to develop measures and to ensure that the correct items are being measured to ensure optimal resource performance and maximum portfolio value.

The portfolio manager should plan to develop and report on a predefined, preapproved set of metrics that monitor strategic goal achievement, financial contribution, stakeholder satisfaction, risk profile, and resource utilization. Metrics measure quantitative or qualitative information aggregated from the portfolio components.

The selected metrics should be relevant to the organizational strategy and objectives and aligned with its other performance metrics. The portfolio management office should be prepared to develop new metrics when appropriate and delete or change metrics that are no longer relevant to the stakeholders or that no longer support the organizational strategy and objectives. The quantity of metrics should not overwhelm the stakeholders to ensure the metrics are actively tracked and understood.

Performance measures and targets (metrics) are set at the portfolio component level and then rolled up to the portfolio level to determine overall portfolio impact. In order to develop meaningful measures, a guideline (often referred to as SMART) is used to ensure performance measures are:

- **Specific.** This provides a clear target as to what is being measured, and the value being realized.
- **Measurable.** The benefits need to be quantifiable, in terms of return on investment, net present value, internal rate of return, payback period, or other organizational value. This should include the methods used to measure, as well as the role and responsibility to obtain the targets as well as value of the portfolio.
- **Attainable.** Measurements are capable of being met with reasonable, even if challenging, effort.
- **Realistic.** The target is achievable, given the organization's capabilities and capacity, that is, it can be challenging but achievable; and
- **Time bound.** There is a time frame set, both for initial targets and metrics, as well as benefit realization.

6.1.2.2   Portfolio Management Information System

A portfolio management information system (PMIS) is a tool, manual or automated, for information collection and distribution to support the portfolio management processes. The PMIS may include costs, performance metrics, risk information, and other information needed to manage and control portfolio performance. The PMIS may provide methods by which internal consistency can be observed and portfolio performance metrics can be collected, monitored, and controlled. The PMIS can also support performance improvement measures.

Portfolio component performance (scope, cost, schedule, and resources) is measured against established baselines to calculate variances that need to be explained. The system may also be used to provide previously used measures and templates for reporting.

The PMIS is often a collection of spreadsheets rather than an automated tool.

6.1.2.4   Capability and Capacity Analysis

This analysis is a technique performed to understand the human, financial, and asset capacity and capability of the organization in order to select, fund, and execute portfolio components. A capability is a specific competency that enables an organization to execute components and deliver results. An appropriate resource management tool, technique, and/or process should be implemented for capturing resource capability and capacity to enable analysis. Resource capability and capacity management analysis may include:

- **Resource types.** The resource types are financial, human resources, physical/intellectual assets, and knowledge bases.
- **Resource schedules.** Resource schedules are histograms combining and detailing forecasts and ongoing resource supply and demand.
- **What-if scenarios.** These scenarios track impacts of portfolio optimization decisions on resource capacity.
- **Finite capacity planning and reporting.** Given the organizational objectives, this planning and reporting tool indicates resource bottlenecks and under and over allocations and is based on priorities that were agreed upon through governance oversight; and performs resource leveling across portfolio components.
- **Resource management tools.** These tools help to quickly and easily identify the resource capability and capacity.

Resource capacity may be analyzed before performance of portfolio resources is included in the portfolio performance management plan.

6.1.3   Develop Portfolio Performance Management Plan: Outputs

6.1.3.1   Portfolio Management Plan Updates

The portfolio performance management plan is a component of or a subsidiary plan of the portfolio management plan. It describes how and when the portfolio resources will be planned, balanced, and allocated to the portfolio components and how the portfolio component progress and resource-related issues and risks are integrated with the resource management activities to ensure that cost-effective resource allocations are made to maximize portfolio performance.

The portfolio performance management plan describes the steps and measures needed to effectively manage portfolio performance as a whole. The plan includes procedures on ways to increase performance levels when performance decreases and procedures for capturing lessons learned for future use.

The plan consists of, but is not limited to, the following:

- Introduction (goals, objectives, strategies, and tactics);
- Performance roles and responsibilities (who will measure and how often);
- Performance measures, that is, what will be measured, which can include metrics on scope, cost, schedule, resources, and benefits);
- Performance reporting (what tools will be used; dissemination of reports, scorecards, and dashboards; and who will be responsible and when);
- Resource optimization (utilization, balancing, and smoothing resource demand against capacity); and
- Benefits realization (how will realized benefits be tracked and compared to plans; how will value be calculated).

One of the critical components of the portfolio performance management plan is benefits realization. The benefits realization planning drills down on the expected benefits for a given portfolio of projects or programs, and details how they will be measured, who will measure them, and when they are measured. Benefits realization planning accomplishes the following:

- Helps to ensure that the benefits of a given portfolio are clearly defined for the stakeholders;
- Documents benefits in such a way that they can be easily measured and evaluated during the course of managing the portfolio; and
- Allows the portfolio's governing bodies to evaluate the expected net benefits of a given portfolio or portfolios to prioritize portfolio efforts. In addition, historical data on actual benefits by previous portfolios can help management make informed decisions when prioritizing future similar components.

The performance planning team works with governing bodies to provide templates and examples for establishing performance measures and targets. The governance team works with the executives to establish and approve these measures and targets. These measures and targets are often called key performance indicators (KPIs) and are used to report whether a particular portfolio is progressing as expected and the results are in line with what the organization expected. In addition, the performance plan looks at future indicators.

For example, in an organization competing for product leadership, the new product pipeline provides a powerful leading performance indication of future sales potential or market share.

6.1.3.2   Portfolio Process Assets Updates

Portfolio process assets that may be updated after completion of planning for portfolio performance include the resource schedule, funding schedule, benefits schedule, and portfolio component schedule.

6.2 Manage Supply and Demand

The required portfolio resources, according to each initiative's business case or plan, should be identified, and an inventory of resources and capabilities should be aggregated at the proper level of detail. This demand is then mapped to existing organizational resources: funds, other tangible and intangible assets, as well as key human resources, such as program and project managers and subject matter experts. A master schedule of resource allocation is necessary to plan the consolidated demand of portfolio resources.

The term "supply" refers to resource capacity including funding and staffing resources as well as equipment and other physical assets shared among portfolio components. "Demand" is the resource requirement from the portfolio components and from the component proposals requesting resources. The goal in managing supply and demand is to ensure resource capacity is optimally allocated against resource requirements or demand based on known organizational priorities and potential value. Resources should be allocated to minimize both unused capacity and unmet demand. The ideal outcome requires diligent, iterative resource management and optimization processes. Figure 6-4 shows the relationship between supply and demand.

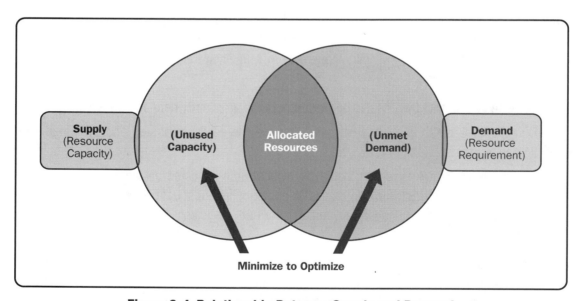

Figure 6-4. Relationship Between Supply and Demand

There are two primary approaches to balancing supply and demand. Some organizations may assume unlimited resources, and resources can be procured through various channels to meet any demand. These are typically projectized organizations. Other organizations are resource-constrained, where resources can be available within a range of variability. These organizations are more often functional or matrix organizations. In functional and matrix organizations, labor resources often are utilized on both project work and operational work. Fluctuations in operational workload will have an impact on the availability of resources for work managed within the portfolio.

There is a complex relationship between the types of resource supplies. The capability and productivity of human resources, even when training, background, and experience are equitable can vary widely. Labor rates can vary based on skill set, experience, industry, and physical location of the resources. Labor resources can be hired or contracted. Equipment and physical assets can be purchased or leased and made available locally or remotely.

Every organization has bottleneck resources, which are skill sets needed on many projects but are in short supply. Bottleneck resources are typically those with an understanding of the business processes, and they also have technical or functional knowledge with the ability to translate business requirements and evaluate the impact of changes. These are skill sets that are difficult to hire or contract due to their scarcity and specific organizational knowledge required. Specialized equipment or facilities can also be bottleneck resources. The demand for these resources needs to be managed continuously. It can be difficult to accurately determine the demand for resources across a portfolio of projects, programs, and operations, at a point in the life cycle before detailed planning has occurred. As portfolio components are selected and planning is conducted, new information regarding resource requirements is often learned.

In order to maximize the use of resources, organizations will commit resources to authorized portfolio components, based on the expected end date of an active portfolio component (commonly referred to as "soft booking"). Unexpected delays or unrecognized dependencies between portfolio components can result in situations where a resource is not available when expected.

Continual and ongoing monitoring of the supply and demand relationship is critical to the success of the portfolio. Information regarding resource utilization and changing resource requirements of active portfolio components as well as the resource needs for planned and approved portfolio components are analyzed against the availability of resources. Then the resources are allocated in a way so that the right resources may be identified and matched to the right projects at the right time. When resources are constrained, the organization is unable to accomplish planned components and may need to reprioritize. Figure 6-5 shows the inputs, tools and techniques, and outputs. Figure 6-6 shows the data flow diagram.

Figure 6-5. Manage Supply and Demand: Inputs, Tools and Techniques, and Outputs

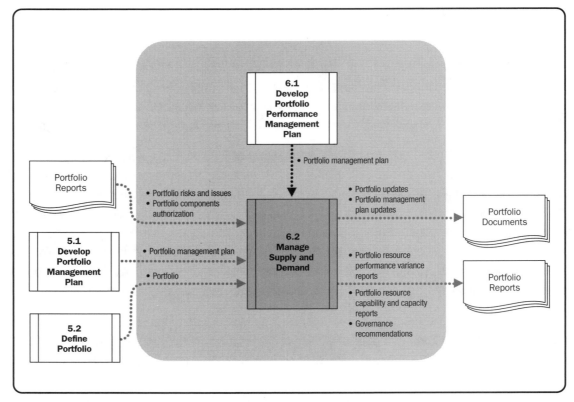

Figure 6-6. Manage Supply and Demand: Data Flow Diagram

6.2.1   Manage Supply and Demand: Inputs

6.2.1.1   Portfolio

The portfolio of active and planned portfolio components represents resource requirements or demand. These requirements are balanced against the resource pool or capacity to determine how best to meet the needs of the portfolio using limited resources. Components are prioritized to help guide resource allocation.

6.2.1.2   Portfolio Management Plan

The portfolio management plan defines how the portfolio will be executed, monitored, and controlled to meet organizational strategy and objectives. The plan provides the high-level guidelines for reporting risks, communicating with the portfolio management team, engaging stakeholders, recommending portfolio component changes, such as delays due to constraints on resources, and other elements.

6.2.1.3 Portfolio Reports

Reports are used for analyzing and managing supply and demand and may include resource utilization reports, vacation schedules, reports on any related equipment or software delivery and/or availability, and financial reports to show funding updates.

6.2.2 Manage Supply and Demand: Tools and Techniques

6.2.2.1 Scenario Analysis

Scenario analysis is necessary to determine various possibilities of resource allocations and the impact to component schedules. Analysis may be used to determine what would happen if human, financial, or equipment funding was increased or decreased, or if constrained resources were not available as scheduled. This type of analysis is important to ensure that the organization is prepared for changes in demand or changes to resource supplies. Organizations need to position themselves to absorb these changes with minimal organizational impact.

Resource management tools are also available for modeling alternative scenarios for using resources to meet the demand of portfolio component priorities.

6.2.2.2 Quantitative and Qualitative Analysis

Quantitative and qualitative analysis includes various approaches to studying the demand for resources against capacity and constraints to determine how to best allocate resources. When bottleneck resources or resource downtime are identified, resource leveling or project sequencing techniques can be applied. Resource leveling strives to smooth performance levels by managing bottleneck areas and communicating delayed schedules if necessary. Recommended changes, requests for more resources, and updates are communicated to the governing body when resource leveling does not produce sufficient results.

The qualitative analysis, dependency analysis, review of resource schedules, and making changes to improve capacity becomes quantitative when working with the number of full-time equivalents (FTEs) required and when determining how many hours need to be allocated for each component, etc.

Trend analysis, using historical data, may also be performed to determine if resource requirements have been consistently underestimated or if resources are consistently over or under performing and adjustments need to be made.

Following the analysis, an organization can take appropriate action based on the drivers of the portfolio. When demand is the primary driver, the organization needs to adjust the resource supply (through temporary and permanent resources). When resource supply is relatively fixed, the organization needs to manage the project demand and sequence project work based on resource availability and project priority. In many cases, organizations will both adjust the resource supply as well as manage project demand.

6.2.2.3 Capability and Capacity Analysis

This analysis will study the capability of resources (e.g., skill sets and certifications), match them against the portfolio's objectives and goals, and translate the capability into what capacity is possible to meet the portfolio demands.

6.2.3 Manage Supply and Demand: Outputs

6.2.3.1 Portfolio Updates

Portfolio resource allocations and schedules may be updated as a result of supply and demand analysis. Recommendations may be presented to the governing body to make changes to the portfolio component mix based on resource capabilities.

6.2.3.2 Portfolio Management Plan Updates

The portfolio management plan includes the approach to resource management planning. Analysis completed during this process may result in recommendations to update resource management strategies in the portfolio management plan.

6.2.3.3 Portfolio Reports

Resource utilization or resource efficiency reports indicate whether resource capacity has been optimally matched against resource demands and highlights areas that need adjustment.

Burn-down or burn-up charts, funnel charts, bubble charts, histograms, and other types of diagrams are useful to show the execution of the portfolio against the overall budget, strategic plan, or other attribute. Other reports may demonstrate the effect of making alternative scenario resource decisions. The goal is for the right resources to be assigned to the right portfolio components at the right time. The reports help the governing body make informed decisions on resources to best achieve organizational objectives.

6.3 Manage Portfolio Value

Portfolio value for an organization can be expressed in multiple ways, including by revenue growth, increased operating margins, employee or customer satisfaction, contribution to the community, enhancement or protection of reputation and branding, and protection of environmental resources. Portfolio value is defined as the aggregate value delivered by the portfolio components, and the goal is to deliver the maximum value possible aligned with strategic objectives and with an acceptable level of risk based on the risk tolerance of the organization.

The method of defining value can differ among organizations. A value measurement framework is often helpful in organizing the value that is to be created, how value will be measured, and recognizing the possible types of value, including both tangible and intangible benefits. The measurement framework facilitates comparison of expected value across the various components and supports informed portfolio decision making for authorizing those components with the maximum expected net value to the organization. The net value considers the expected gross benefits or value minus the required investment of time and resources.

During the optimization process, component proposals provide initial assessments of expected business value and the (often intangible) contributions to organizational objectives. The expected value to be returned by the portfolio component is a significant attribute of the weighting and scoring leading to authorization. Once authorized, accountability for delivering the consequent value is assigned. Also, expected value will continue to be measured throughout the component's life cycle.

The expected value of components can change as portfolio components are planned, developed, and executed. Changes in actual scope, schedule, cost, or performance can affect the expected value. External factors such as market conditions, competitor actions, laws and regulations, risks realized, and other factors can also affect whether the expected value at delivery of the products, services, or assets created or enhanced has changed.

As components are completed and the organization begins to realize the consequential benefits and value, measures are again taken to ensure that the intended benefits are gained and value is realized. The process to formally measure achieved portfolio value against expected portfolio value ensures that the portfolio continues to drive the correct work into the portfolio, organizational objectives are being achieved, and estimates for value are being established correctly in the component proposals. The value measurement framework is continuously improved by lessons learned through execution.

Outputs from this process include recommendations for changes to the portfolio and information to enable more effective and efficient decision making in the organization.

Figure 6-7 shows the inputs, tools and techniques, and outputs. Figure 6-8 shows the data flow diagram.

Figure 6-7. Manage Portfolio Value: Inputs, Tools and Techniques, and Outputs

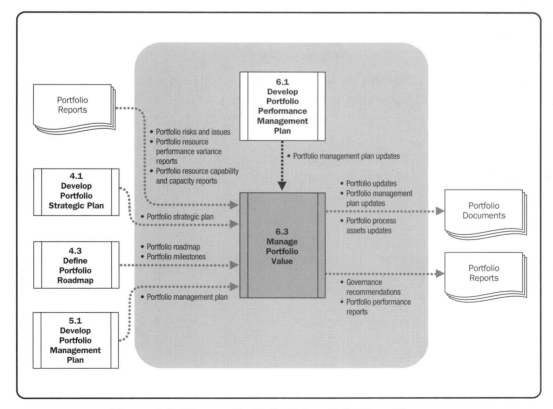

Figure 6-8. Manage Portfolio Value: Data Flow Diagram

6.3.1 Manage Portfolio Value: Inputs

6.3.1.1 Portfolio Roadmap

The portfolio roadmap provides a high-level timeline for expected portfolio component delivery. Delays in scheduled delivery of one or more portfolio components can have a ripple effect through the portfolio, effecting resource utilization, and initiation of other portfolio components. Delays in delivery of portfolio component results may adversely affect the value derived from the portfolio.

6.3.1.2 Portfolio Management Plan

The portfolio management plan provides for the continual identification and assessment of the value of the portfolio benefits and the impact on the organizational objectives, identification and monitoring of the interdependencies between the benefits being delivered by the various portfolio components, analysis of the potential impact of planned portfolio component changes on benefits outcome, and assignment of responsibilities and accountability for the actual realization of benefits provided by the portfolio components.

6.3.1.3 Portfolio Reports

Portfolio reports include reports of aggregate portfolio component performance (time, cost, and scope), progress against plans, updated forecasts of expected value to be delivered, and variance reports.

Portfolio performance variance reports aggregate portfolio component data and compare the original expected value contribution of the combined portfolio to the current expected value contribution based on changes to the portfolio components, various internal and external risk factors, and competitor and market data, among other factors.

Performance variance/alert techniques should support content and be in a format that is standardized across all portfolio components. Simple burn-down or burn-up charts showing the delivery of a component compared to the portfolio's budget or time is a simple representation of progress. A common representation includes visual indicators, such as the traffic light colors (red, yellow, green, and sometimes blue to indicate completed portfolio components), which signify levels of portfolio component performance. Figure 6-9 shows an example with milestone markers displayed where schedules were exceeded or missed.

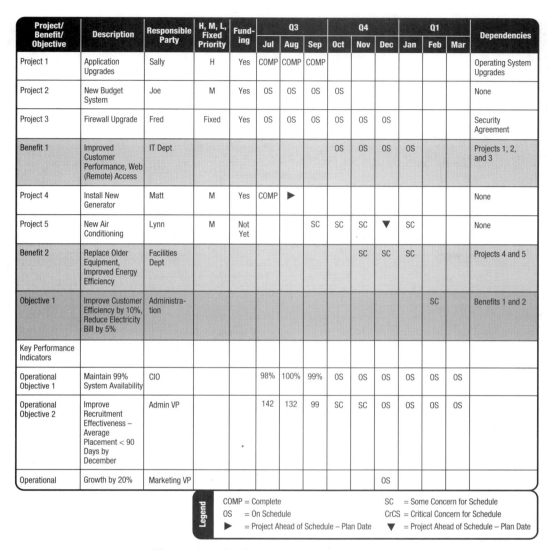

Project/ Benefit/ Objective	Description	Responsible Party	H, M, L, Fixed Priority	Fund-ing	Q3			Q4			Q1			Dependencies
					Jul	Aug	Sep	Oct	Nov	Dec	Jan	Feb	Mar	
Project 1	Application Upgrades	Sally	H	Yes	COMP	COMP	COMP							Operating System Upgrades
Project 2	New Budget System	Joe	M	Yes	OS	OS	OS	OS						None
Project 3	Firewall Upgrade	Fred	Fixed	Yes	OS	OS	OS	OS	OS	OS				Security Agreement
Benefit 1	Improved Customer Performance, Web (Remote) Access	IT Dept						OS	OS	OS	OS			Projects 1, 2, and 3
Project 4	Install New Generator	Matt	M	Yes	COMP	▶								None
Project 5	New Air Conditioning	Lynn	M	Not Yet			SC	SC	SC	▼	SC			None
Benefit 2	Replace Older Equipment, Improved Energy Efficiency	Facilities Dept							SC	SC	SC			Projects 4 and 5
Objective 1	Improve Customer Efficiency by 10%, Reduce Electricity Bill by 5%	Administra-tion										SC		Benefits 1 and 2
Key Performance Indicators														
Operational Objective 1	Maintain 99% System Availability	CIO			98%	100%	99%	OS	OS	OS	OS	OS	OS	
Operational Objective 2	Improve Recruitment Effectiveness – Average Placement < 90 Days by December	Admin VP			142	132	99	SC	SC	OS	OS	OS	OS	
Operational	Growth by 20%	Marketing VP							OS					

Legend
COMP = Complete   SC = Some Concern for Schedule
OS = On Schedule   CrCS = Critical Concern for Schedule
▶ = Project Ahead of Schedule – Plan Date   ▼ = Project Ahead of Schedule – Plan Date

Figure 6-9. Performance Variance Report

6.3.2   Manage Portfolio Value: Tools and Techniques

The Manage Portfolio Value process tools and techniques provide ways to analyze the various inputs to determine how portfolio value is affected by recent changes. The tools and techniques also provide the means to identify what might be done to positively affect the portfolio value in light of the multitude of factors.

This process is an enabler for the portfolio optimization and authorization processes as it ensures portfolio components and their benefits can be easily compared to one another based on carefully selected, consistently applied value criteria. Sample benefits criteria include strategic alignment, customer satisfaction, financial return, asset usage efficiency, mandated compliance, and organizational process improvement. These criteria should allow for tracking planned value once the contributing components are completed. Benefits may be categorized and the categories can be prioritized. The relationships between components, their resulting benefits and the outcomes can be managed on a schedule as shown in Figure 6-10.

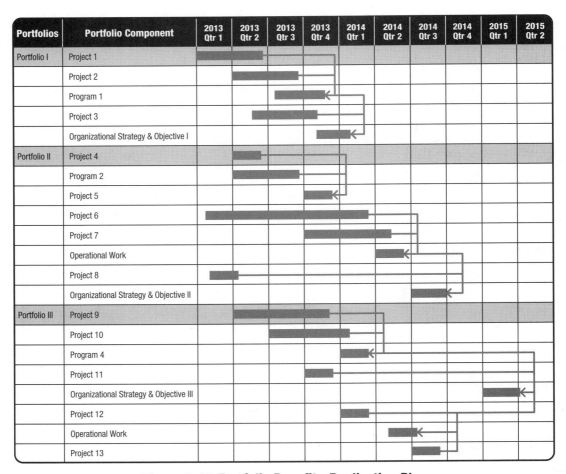

Portfolios	Portfolio Component	2013 Qtr 1	2013 Qtr 2	2013 Qtr 3	2013 Qtr 4	2014 Qtr 1	2014 Qtr 2	2014 Qtr 3	2014 Qtr 4	2015 Qtr 1	2015 Qtr 2
Portfolio I	Project 1										
	Project 2										
	Program 1										
	Project 3										
	Organizational Strategy & Objective I										
Portfolio II	Project 4										
	Program 2										
	Project 5										
	Project 6										
	Project 7										
	Operational Work										
	Project 8										
	Organizational Strategy & Objective II										
Portfolio III	Project 9										
	Project 10										
	Program 4										
	Project 11										
	Organizational Strategy & Objective III										
	Project 12										
	Operational Work										
	Project 13										

Figure 6-10. Portfolio Benefits-Realization Plan

6.3.2.1   Elicitation Techniques

Elicitation techniques used in the Manage Portfolio Value process include meeting with the stakeholders to assess criteria and to discern the weight assigned to different benefits and outcomes. SWOT analysis (strengths, weaknesses, opportunities, and threats) can also be used to elicit information to ensure benefits are comprehensively and holistically taken into consideration. Benefits result from exploiting a strength or opportunity as well as from positively addressing a weakness or threat.

6.3.2.2   Value Scoring and Measurement Analysis

There are various methods that can be used to score and measure the organizational value:

- **Scoring models.** Scoring models may be used to consistently document and assess financially intangible portfolio benefits (those benefits that cannot be assessed using financial return on investment methods). All criteria in the benefits scoring model should relate to organizational priorities. Using a scoring model facilitates agreement as to what is important and ensures the criteria is documented and applied consistently to all intangible benefits.

A simple way to show scoring of a component against criteria is shown in Figure 6-11.

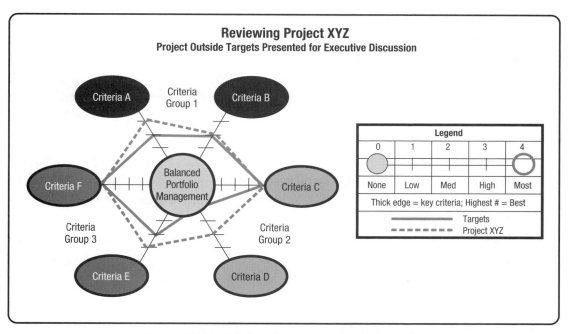

Figure 6-11. Scoring Component Performance

When conditions change, an updated analysis may show a need to revise criteria weights. The example in Figure 6-12 shows that strategic changes (shown as dark ovals at Criteria A and Criteria B) call for changes to the original weighting to occur (shown as dark circles against Criteria A and Criteria E), due to new organization conditions. This causes reweighting of two of the six criteria used for portfolio management by the impacted organization.

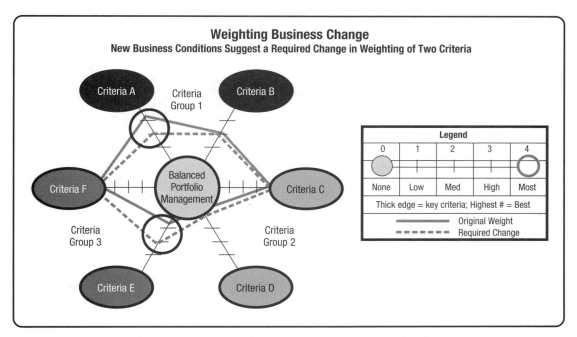

Figure 6-12. Changes in the Weighting for Scoring Performance

- **Cost-Benefit Analysis.** This analysis seeks to define the benefits that will be provided by the portfolio and compare it to the costs of the portfolio. Benefits may be financial, such as increased profits, but may also be nonfinancial such as increased market share or a new capability. The cost-benefit analysis should be tracked and reevaluated as required throughout portfolio performance management, as the portfolio component changes or as the financial or competitive environment changes. Return on investment and net present value (the present value of inflows minus the present values of outflows) are helpful in determining expected impact.

- **Comparative Advantage Analysis.** When conducting comparative advantage analysis against a strategic objective or portfolio component proposal, it is important to consider that competing efforts may reside within or external to the organization. A typical component proposal includes some level of analysis and comparison against current or future alternatives. This technique may also include conducting a what-if analysis to consider how the portfolio component and its intended benefits could be achieved by various options, including resource capability and capacity mix.

- **Progress measurement techniques.** The tools and techniques used at the portfolio level are similar to those used in a portfolio component such as earned value.

- **Value measurement techniques.** Performance indicators are defined based on assessed value and are used to measure and report portfolio performance.

- **Portfolio Efficient Frontier.** The efficient frontier (see Figure 6-13) is based on Harry Markowitz's Modern Portfolio Theory and gives the decision makers the analytical tool to optimize portfolios given the resource constraints. The portfolio, is referred to as "efficient" if it has the best possible expected level of return for its level of risk (usually proxied by the standard deviation of the portfolio's

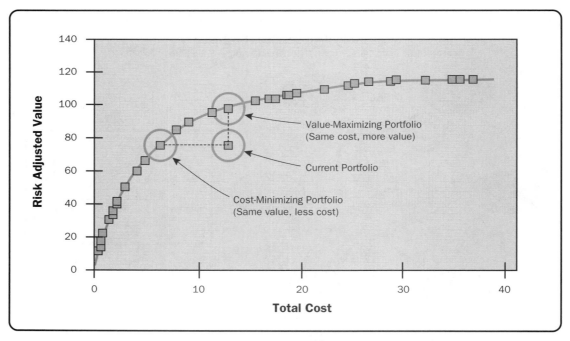

Figure 6-13. Portfolio Efficient Frontier

return). Diversification may allow for the same portfolio expected return with reduced risk. It should be noted that efficient frontiers are not static and organizations should monitor cost-benefit ratios on a continual basis.

6.3.2.3 Benefits Realization Analysis

Organization benefits and value expand beyond economic value (also known as economic profit, economic value added, and shareholder value) to include other forms of value such as employee value, customer value, supplier value, channel partner value, alliance partner value, managerial value, and societal value. Many of these forms of value are not directly measured in monetary terms.

A number of tools can help an organization increase their achievement of planned benefits:

- **Results chain.** A results chain shows the cause and effect relationships between the portfolio components that are needed to deliver planned benefits. The relationships show a series of sequenced benefits that are needed to achieve planned outcomes and develop the value to the organization. This tool is used to identify the specific contributions that each portfolio component makes to the overall portfolio value. It also shows gaps and overlaps that need to be addressed to more effectively or efficiently realize planned benefits.

- **Outcome probability analysis of the portfolio.** The portfolio manager estimates the potential portfolio outcomes with respect to success criteria, listing the possible values of the corresponding performance indicators with their associated confidence levels. This output is typically expressed as a cumulative distribution (see Figure 6-14) that the project manager can use to set realistic targets in line with stakeholder risk tolerances.

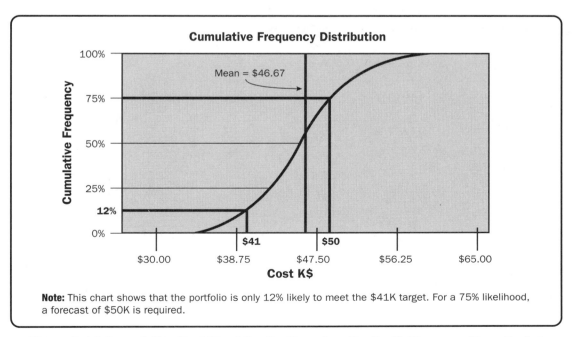

Figure 6-14. Cumulative Cost Chart for the Spend on the Portfolio over a Given Period

Various other methods can be used to both visualize and aid the management of portfolio benefits depending on the situation and requirements involved, for example, various graphical methods such as charts showing planned vs. actual targets.

6.3.3 Manage Portfolio Value: Outputs

The outputs of the Manage Portfolio Value process provide critical information needed to perform ongoing portfolio optimization and authorization.

6.3.3.1 Portfolio Management Plan Updates

The portfolio management plan may be updated to identify new reporting, new measures, or other processes by which the portfolio and the current portfolio components will be managed. This may include new measures to be collected and analyzed, new reports to be created and distributed, or changes in roles and responsibilities for managing the portfolio.

6.3.3.2 Portfolio Reports

Portfolio reports provide information about the performance and forecasts of the portfolio. These reports also include variances, analysis of the variances, and recommendations to be considered by the governing body. If there are savings forecasted in the components, these reports may be used as a source of information for adjusting the subsequent year's budget.

6.3.3.3 Portfolio Process Assets Updates

Lessons learned that are collected and analyzed may provide ways to heighten efficiency or effectiveness, resulting in updates to best practice descriptions, training guides, and educational documentation and standards for policy, process, procedures, or tools for managing value.

7

PORTFOLIO COMMUNICATION MANAGEMENT

The Portfolio Communication Management Knowledge Area includes the processes to develop the portfolio communication management plan and manage portfolio information. Portfolio communication management processes are closely aligned with strategic, governance, performance, and risk management processes.

Selecting a communication strategy is focused on satisfying the most important information needs of stakeholders so that effective portfolio decisions are made and organizational objectives are met. Transparency may be a communication strategy to mitigate the risk of inadequate communication. Transparency with priorities and status may provide credibility for the portfolio manager, establish good relationships with stakeholders, and help reduce the chance of resources working on efforts not aligned with the organizational strategy and objectives.

The Portfolio Communications Management processes are (see Figure 7-1 for overview):

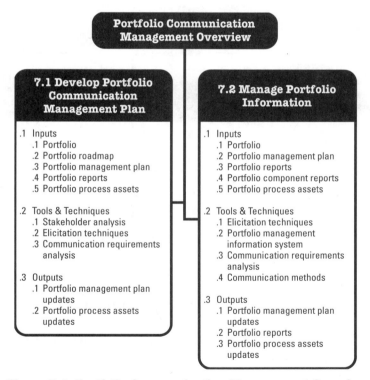

Figure 7-1. Portfolio Communication Management Overview

7.1 Develop Portfolio Communication Management Plan—Includes portfolio stakeholders' identification as well as planning effective solutions to satisfy the communication requirements.

7.2 Manage Portfolio Information—Executes the communication plan by collecting data, translating data into meaningful information, and supplying it to the identified stakeholders in a timely and effective manner.

7.1 Develop Portfolio Communication Management Plan

Figure 7-2 provides an overview of communication management including stakeholder and communication requirements analysis, the focus of consultation and participation of stakeholders for identifying risks, and the flow and input of communication management to portfolio information and reporting. The management of portfolio information is described in Section 7.2.

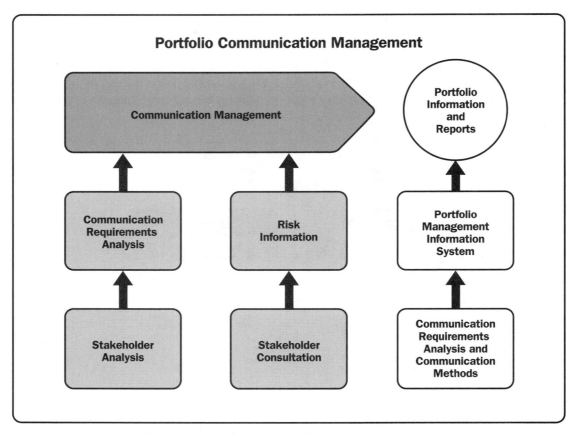

Figure 7-2. Portfolio Communication Management

Portfolio communication facilitates a two-way effective dialogue between affected internal and external stakeholders, individuals, or groups, including:

- Executive managers,
- Operations managers,
- Governing bodies,

- Sponsors,

- Project/program/portfolio managers,

- Suppliers and external resource providers,

- Regulatory bodies, and

- Others.

In order to develop the portfolio communication management plan, stakeholder identification and analysis is necessary in addition to the determination of communication requirements.

In planning portfolio communication, the portfolio management plan may identify some of the primary stakeholders, such as executive managers and sponsors, who are accountable for the success of the portfolio. Planning may uncover additional stakeholders that require or benefit from the knowledge of portfolio progress, performance, and changes. These additional discoveries are reflected as updates to the portfolio management plan. As a comprehensive list of stakeholders is compiled, it is important to determine their information needs and the preferred mode of communication. Developing a strong communication management plan requires inputs from a variety of other portfolio management processes, such as performance and risk management.

Portfolio communication recognizes the broad and varied stakeholders from executive management through individuals performing the basic tasks to third parties. The information needs of portfolio stakeholders are much more varied than with project-level communication primarily because of the breadth and variety of stakeholders. Transparency in planning portfolio management reporting is important for discovering early if elements are missing and to manage risk due to insufficient or inconsistent communication. Transparent communication is also valuable when planning for optimal utilization of resources.

Figure 7-3 shows the inputs, tools and techniques, and outputs. Figure 7-4 shows the data flow diagram.

Figure 7-3. Develop Portfolio Communication Management Plan: Inputs, Tools and Techniques, and Outputs

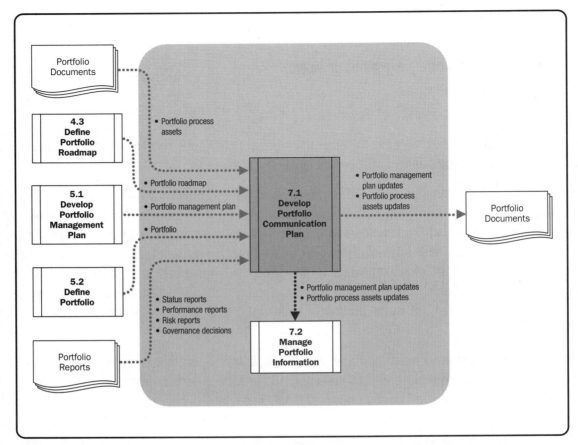

Figure 7-4. Develop Portfolio Communication Management Plan: Data Flow Diagram

7.1.1 Develop Portfolio Communication Management Plan: Inputs

7.1.1.1 Portfolio

The portfolio includes the list of approved and potential portfolio components as well as other descriptive information on the components such as dependencies, level of effort, points of contact, and other dashboard-type information. Knowledge of the components of the portfolio may have an effect on the communication approach used for consolidating and standardizing communication and evaluating communication strategy at a portfolio (as opposed to a component) level. The portfolio list of components is critical in understanding the full scope of communication needed.

7.1.1.2 Portfolio Roadmap

The portfolio roadmap helps with the understanding of the structure of the portfolio, interdependencies among the portfolio components, and how all of the portfolio components "fit together" in order to lay out the plan for achieving organizational strategy and objectives. Clear and timely communication of this roadmap and any changes to the roadmap is a fundamental part of portfolio communication. The portfolio communication management plan may include information about interdependencies among the portfolio's components that could impact portfolio communication objectives.

7.1.1.3 Portfolio Management Plan

The portfolio management plan provides the scope of the portfolio and the initial list of primary internal and external portfolio stakeholders including the governance model. The portfolio management plan is the guiding artifact that establishes portfolio-level dependencies and constraints to allow for effective oversight. The portfolio management plan describes the planned approach for approving, prioritizing, and scheduling the portfolio components and setting priorities. All elements of the portfolio management plan have communication requirements, such as risks that need to be communicated to the governing body, the portfolio manager, and the stakeholders. Changes in the portfolio management plan may introduce new stakeholders or new communication requirements.

The communication management plan may be a subsidiary plan to the portfolio management plan or may be included within the portfolio management plan.

7.1.1.4 Portfolio Reports

Portfolio reports include a variety of reports, such as portfolio status or progress reports, performance reports, portfolio risk reports, and summary reports from the overall governance of portfolio components. Portfolio performance reports can provide information on the total investment in each portfolio component, which serves as the communication of assessed portfolio value. Some organizations communicate with dashboards to provide status information at a glance. The format and content of these reports should be defined in the portfolio communication management plan providing templates, standard forms, and procedures for planned portfolio reporting.

7.1.1.5 Portfolio Process Assets

Portfolio process assets related to planning portfolio communication include:

- Portfolio manager roles and responsibilities,
- Status reports,
- Portfolio risk profile or risk assessment with key risks and issues,
- Portfolio forecasts with variance to plan,
- Governance decisions,
- Funding decisions,
- Resource decisions,
- Portfolio value assessments, and
- Delegations of responsibility for communication.

7.1.2 Develop Portfolio Communication Management Plan: Tools and Techniques

7.1.2.1 Stakeholder Analysis

The purpose of stakeholder analysis is to identify the stakeholders, determine the different individuals and groups, and determine their concerns, interests, and influence. For portfolio management, it is important to understand the stakeholder's interest and influence in the portfolio investment in order to develop the portfolio communication management plan. After gathering information about who the portfolio stakeholders are, the process of stakeholder analysis captures information about each stakeholder and the relationships among them. Stakeholder analysis also includes stakeholder classification.

In stakeholder identification, a list of all stakeholders is made. Attributes of the stakeholders are gathered, such as which stakeholder group they are a part of. Stakeholder groups are defined in Section 2.7. Stakeholders in the same group may have different concerns and interests, and stakeholder concerns and interests may change over time. In addition to classifying them in groups, stakeholders are classified as either external or internal, as shown in Table 7-1.

Table 7-1. Types of Stakeholders

Portfolio Stakeholders	
External Portfolio Stakeholders	The interest, influence, and communication needs of business partners, competitors, government, industry, legal, customers, investors, shareholders and public relations as it relates to the overall portfolio and the individual changes being managed.
Internal Portfolio Stakeholders	The interest, influence, and communication needs of business operational stakeholders who are looking to ensure alignment between portfolio components, while minimizing negative impact and maximizing positive benefits of all portfolio-managed changes to their business operations.

The stakeholders who need to be informed consistently about the status of the portfolio include: the internal stakeholders who have interest in or influence the delivery of business change, external stakeholders who are outside the scope of the portfolio but can influence or need communication from the portfolio, sponsors who are owners of the portfolio components, and the portfolio manager.

Assigning stakeholders into groups and classifying them as external or internal helps to target the optimal type of communication and whether various communications can be grouped to match the stakeholder grouping. In addition, once grouped, analysis can be done on that group's ability to influence the portfolio. For assessing influence, the following questions may be asked:

- Who are the members of the governing body? Are there governance processes to be supported, such as portfolio component proposal validations, ROI considerations, and investment management practices? How do these processes affect information requirements (i.e., who needs what information)?

- Which of the stakeholders are thought leaders, influencers, or early adopters? Which stakeholders are known to resist change? Do they support or undermine each other's change initiatives?

- What level of authority does each stakeholder have affecting the portfolio and the organization?

- What is their political influence in the organization?

- Is their role as a stakeholder recognized by the organization?

- What are the interrelationships among the stakeholders?

- Which of the stakeholders can significantly influence others?

After assigning levels of influence, stakeholder analysis is also performed to assess the level of interest and urgency in communication by each stakeholder.

A simple way of devising a stakeholder communication management strategy, based on this analysis, is to use influence and interest levels mapped to quadrants. If a stakeholder has low interest in the reports coming out of the communication, for example, and has a low level of influence and authority, the strategy may be to plan to minimize the effort in reaching this stakeholder. Figure 7-5 provides an example of these concepts.

Setting Stakeholder Communication Strategy			
		Level of Interest	
		Low	High
Level of Influence	Low	Apply minimal effort	Keep informed
	High	Active communications	Active communications and engagement

Figure 7-5. Stakeholder Communication Strategy Matrix

An understanding of the core communication needs of each stakeholder is also necessary for planning. What kind of information is each stakeholder interested in and what type of communication do they expect to ensure portfolio success? Refer to Table 7-2 for an example of a stakeholder matrix used in stakeholder analysis.

Table 7-2. Stakeholder Matrix for Use in Stakeholder Analysis

Stakeholder Groups	Stakeholder Roles	Stakeholder Interests	Stakeholder Expectations
Portfolio Sponsors	• Provides funding • Provides resources • Provides high-level scoping	• Benefits and outcomes that meet the organization's goals	• To be informed regularly of portfolio return on investment, key portfolio milestones, risks, costs, and schedule
Portfolio Governance	• Oversees the portfolio • Sets priorities • Manages the spending • Reports progress • Manages timely delivery of benefits	• Portfolio performance • Governance decisions • Change decisions • Concerns of sponsors and governing body	• To be the most knowledgeable party of portfolio progress against goals • To be aware of all developments of consequence
PMO	• Ensures that portfolio management best practices are being followed	• Project progress • Lessons learned • Developing PMO materials for future use	• To receive notification of all portfolio changes and portfolio needs
Contract Management Team (vendors, legal)	• Ensures that funding is intact • Manages the contract • Ensures efficient availability of contractor staff	• Financial standings • Project progress • Contract impacts and changes	• To be made aware of progress against contractual deliverables • To be made aware of any changes to the contract including increased resource requirements
Portfolio Component Teams	• Report progress and completion of components	• Portfolio changes • Portfolio risks and issues	• To receive notification of all portfolio changes, risks, and issues

7.1.2.2 Elicitation Techniques

As portfolio stakeholders and stakeholder communication requirements change over time, it is important for the portfolio manager to engage with stakeholders to ensure their needs are being met and are aligned with the communication management plan. This may be achieved through interviews, questionnaires/surveys, stakeholder meetings, and lessons learned sessions on the effectiveness of communication.

By meeting with stakeholders, for example, the portfolio manager can review the planned communication to get feedback on the plan. Brainstorming can be helpful in identifying new stakeholder groups previously not considered, and in these meetings, portfolio stakeholders can confirm or change the communication requirements.

7.1.2.3 Communication Requirements Analysis

In communication requirements analysis, the vehicle or tool used to communicate information to the stakeholders and the frequency planned is evaluated to determine if changes should be made. A list of available communication methods are charted to evaluate alternatives and ensure the optimal vehicle is being used to meet stakeholder needs.

Reviews are conducted to identify any redundant communication. Some redundancy is intentional to ensure reaching multiple types of recipients or when intended recipients have varied preferences for receiving information. Choices may need to be made to identify which communication is primary and which should be discontinued.

A communication matrix may be used for capturing and recording the results of this analysis. Table 7-3 is an example of a communication matrix. This document is foundational to building the communication management plan.

Table 7-3. Communication Matrix

Communication Areas	Frequency	Intended Recipient	Communication Vehicles*
Portfolio Governance Decisions	Quarterly and monthly	Project sponsors Portfolio manager PMO Contracting officer	Quarterly and monthly reports on internal portal
Portfolio Dashboard	Weekly	Project sponsors Portfolio manager PMO	Governance meetings, email distribution, portfolio dashboards on internal portal
Portfolio Performance Reports	Weekly	Portfolio sponsors Portfolio stakeholders Functional managers	Governance meetings, status reports with email distribution, newsletters, blogs, portfolio dashboards on internal portal
Key Risks and Issues Updates	Weekly	Portfolio sponsors Portfolio stakeholders Functional managers	Governance meetings, status reports with email distribution
Resource Utilization	Weekly	Project team Project team members SMEs	Governance meetings, status reports with email distribution, portfolio dashboards on internal portal

*Multiple vehicles for sending a communication do not necessarily mean redundant communication. Sometimes multiple vehicles are necessary to reach different types of recipients or the recipients have varied preferences for receiving the information.

To complete portfolio communication requirements analysis, an assessment of the organizational culture is helpful to ensure the communication management plan is suitable for the organization. If the organization is generally comfortable with technology, portals may be planned more extensively as the primary vehicle for reporting information. If the organization is not comfortable with technology, they may prefer paper reports and emails. Updates for organizational culture can be reflected in the matrix.

7.1.3 Develop Portfolio Communication Management Plan: Outputs

7.1.3.1 Portfolio Management Plan Updates

The communication management plan may be a subsidiary plan of the portfolio management plan or may be included within the portfolio management plan document. The portfolio communication management plan defines all communication needs, establishes communication requirements, specifies frequency, and identifies recipients for information associated with the portfolio management process.

Stakeholders may require new communication that changes the portfolio management plan. Stakeholder and communication analyses will drive what is intended to be communicated with regard to the portfolio and how it is expected to be communicated. The results of these analyses will be documented in a portfolio communication management plan. This plan defines the expected process for information collection, review, formatting and delivering communication about the portfolio. It also sets expectations among project teams regarding the actions and processes necessary to facilitate the critical alignment among people, ideas, and information, which are necessary for successful portfolio communication. The risk of insufficient communication planning could result in failure to identify risks, accomplish portfolio objectives, increase duplication of effort, and reduce stakeholder confidence. At a minimum, the communication management plan should include:

- Communication objectives,
- Roles and responsibilities for managing communication,
- Identified stakeholders,
- Identified stakeholder expectations,
- Planned methods to collect and store communication,
- Planned vehicles to access and deliver communication,
- Planned frequency, and
- Communication policies/constraints.

7.1.3.2 Portfolio Process Assets Updates

Portfolio process assets updates will be made including updates to communication management roles and responsibilities, policies or procedures, tools or templates, portfolio key risks and issues, and lessons learned for any knowledge gained on the effectiveness of portfolio communication management.

7.2 Manage Portfolio Information

The process to manage portfolio information includes collecting, analyzing, storing, and delivering portfolio information to stakeholders in accordance with their requirements in a timely manner. In managing portfolio information, communication is delivered to the intended audiences through various communication mechanisms. Many communications are also stored for a period of time in portfolio repositories for future access.

When using web portal dashboards to communicate status, processes need to be created and managed to ensure updates are accurate and timely. If the portfolio management capability is not sufficiently mature in the organization, spreadsheets may be used to ensure accuracy for PMIS rather than an automated tool.

Figure 7-6 shows the inputs, tools and techniques, and outputs. Figure 7-7 shows the data flow diagram.

Inputs	Tools & Techniques	Outputs
.1 Portfolio .2 Portfolio management plan .3 Portfolio reports .4 Portfolio component reports .5 Portfolio process assets	.1 Elicitation techniques .2 Portfolio management information system .3 Communication requirements analysis .4 Communication methods	.1 Portfolio management plan updates .2 Portfolio reports .3 Portfolio process assets updates

Figure 7-6. Manage Portfolio Information: Inputs, Tools and Techniques, and Outputs

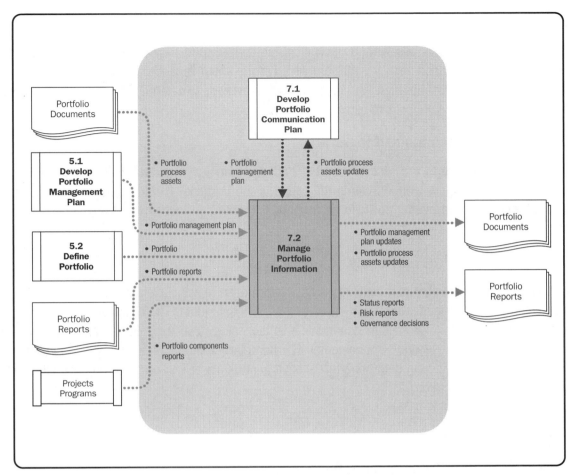

Figure 7-7. Manage Portfolio Information: Data Flow Diagram

7.2.1 Manage Portfolio Information: Inputs

7.2.1.1 Portfolio

The portfolio is a list of components whose updates are needed for communication to several stakeholder audiences. New components added to the portfolio may translate to new sets of stakeholders and new stakeholder communication requirements.

7.2.1.2 Portfolio Management Plan

The portfolio management plan provides the intended approach for managing the portfolio, stakeholder expectations and requirements, communication management, performance, and risks. This plan is used in managing communication to ensure all communication action plans are aligned with processes defined in the portfolio management plan. For example, if the portfolio management plan mentions that portfolio component proposals for new investments will be reviewed and approved in the governing body meetings, then communication will need to be built around that requirement.

7.2.1.3   Portfolio Reports

Portfolio reports include changes such as cancelled, authorized, and new portfolio component proposals, resource information, governance decisions, performance reports about variances or goal achievement, risk and issue reports, and status. The information from these reports is reviewed to determine what meets the stakeholder requirements and therefore what needs to be communicated.

7.2.1.4   Portfolio Component Reports

Portfolio component reports are received by the portfolio manager regularly as status reports from the program and project managers working within the scope of the portfolio. These reports may be consolidated and evaluated for impact on overall portfolio performance to determine which stakeholders will receive the communication.

7.2.1.5   Portfolio Process Assets

Portfolio process assets related to managing portfolio information may include communication guidelines and procedures, information distribution methods, risks, and performance data. These assets may include portfolio communication requirements (e.g., specific communication technology available, allowed communication media, record retention policies, and security requirements). The portfolio's unique makeup, as well as insights gained from stakeholder analysis, will help determine the relative importance of each asset to the overall approach to managing the portfolio information.

7.2.2   Manage Portfolio Information: Tools and Techniques

7.2.2.1   Elicitation Techniques

Elicitation techniques have been described earlier (see Section 5.1). Elicitation is also used here to collect data and information to be communicated. Data gathering may involve portfolio component review meetings focused on validating and understanding data included in component status reports. Information gathering in the portfolio environment includes gathering strategic program and project data, as well as data and information related to ongoing operations which may interest stakeholders for decision-making purposes.

7.2.2.2   Portfolio Management Information System

A portfolio management information system (PMIS), described in Section 2.5, includes document repository and document version control systems and communication management processes and tools, in addition to other tools and processes required to support portfolio management.

A PMIS provides a technology-based method of capturing and managing all portfolio-related communication needs. An effective portfolio management information system can enable the definition, analysis, design, generation or production, construction, and information management to ensure successful communication management. For communication and information management specifically, the PMIS can store information, summarize it for reporting, and assist in managing communication channels. In less mature organizations, the PMIS may be a collection of spreadsheets or other portfolio documents.

Some PMIS include real-time dashboards that have automated alert systems, which can warn the decision makers or portfolio managers about impending risks, issues, and market dynamics, etc., as soon as the triggering event occurs.

7.2.2.3   Communication Requirements Analysis

Data gathered in the Manage Portfolio Information process often begins as raw data or information without full context. Some of this data may be from external research specifically for market comparative analysis. With this communication requirements analysis technique, the data and information are analyzed to separate the data that hold value to the receiving audience. One way to help make data meaningful is to build forecasts based on trends in the data. Other ways include pulling out select, meaningful data for communicating in newsletters or in news areas on a web portal.

The goal of this analysis is to glean the most meaningful, accurate information, ensure it is delivered in a meaningful format, and match the communication method with the documented stakeholders' requirements. Communicating information effectively promotes knowledge sharing, credibility, and informed management decision making.

7.2.2.4   Communication Methods

Methods to communicate portfolio information will depend upon the context of the portfolio and the needs of the stakeholders. Communication methods may include visual representations of the data and information received such as dashboards, resource histograms, and a communication calendar.

- **Dashboards.** Dashboards are an effective way to communicate multiple messages on portfolio status and trending simultaneously. An example of a dashboard is shown in Figure 7-8.

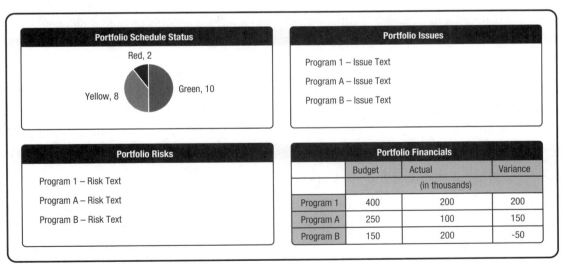

Figure 7-8. Portfolio Dashboard

- **Resource histograms.** Changing organization priorities that realign resource efforts, alter the work force, and modify the cost structure of resources will impact portfolio performance. The portfolio manager needs to determine if the resulting impact(s) are value-added or adverse to portfolio performance. A resource histogram is a graphical representation of this information. This type of representation will aid in identifying portfolio risk associated with resource over- or under-allocations across the portfolio.

- **Communication calendar.** The communication calendar is a representation of all of the communication for the portfolio and their frequency over a period of time. It takes into account all of the existing communication dependencies associated with the portfolio as well as the time-sensitive needs of the stakeholders. For example, if a monthly finance reporting meeting occurs on the fifth day of each month, this could create a predecessor portfolio review meeting to prepare outputs for the financial organization to meet a deadline.

7.2.3 Manage Portfolio Information: Outputs

7.2.3.1 Portfolio Management Plan Updates

During the manage portfolio information process, new communication or information management needs and methods may be determined. These updates are included in the contents of the portfolio management plan or the subsidiary communication management plan.

7.2.3.2 Portfolio Reports

Information management activities related to portfolio reporting will change based on evolving stakeholder needs, collection and storage methods, as well as retrieval and delivery mechanisms. The portfolio reports will change based on the availability of information for critical decision making, identification of trends, and improvement in the speed and quality of information. Types of communication reports include announcements in stakeholder meetings, email communication, blogs, dashboards, web portal postings, portfolio manager meetings, and exception reporting cycles when significant changes occur in the portfolio.

Managing information and communication should focus on the proactive and targeted development and delivery of key messages and engagement of stakeholders at the right time and in the right manner. Communication of proposed strategic changes to a portfolio may often cross organizational and department boundaries to secure agreement.

7.2.3.3 Portfolio Process Assets Updates

Portfolio process assets updates are made to various information management policies, procedures, guidelines, and distribution methods. These updates may include portfolio risks and issues, key stakeholders, meeting minutes, and status reports where the communication requirements analysis has produced new information and changes are required.

8

PORTFOLIO RISK MANAGEMENT

Portfolio risk is an uncertain event or condition that, if it occurs, has a positive or negative effect on one or more project objectives. A risk may have one or more causes and, if it occurs, the corresponding effects may have a positive or negative impact on one or more portfolio success criteria. An overview of the portfolio risk management processes is provided in Figure 8-1.

Figure 8-1. Portfolio Risk Management Overview

Risk management is a structured process for assessing and analyzing portfolio risks with the goal of capitalizing on the potential opportunities and mitigating those events, activities, or circumstances which can adversely impact the portfolio. Risk management is critical where interdependencies exist between high-priority portfolio components, where the cost of portfolio component failure is significant, or when risks from one portfolio component raise the risks in another portfolio component. Risk management identifies and exploits the potential improvements in portfolio component performance that may increase quality, customer satisfaction, service levels, and productivity for both the portfolio components and the organization. Risk management may generate new portfolio components as well.

The objective of portfolio risk management is to accept the right amount of risk commensurate with the anticipated reward to deliver the optimum outcomes for the organization in the short, medium, and longer term. Portfolio risk management differs from project and program risk management in that, in the right circumstances at the portfolio level, the organization may choose to actively embrace appropriate risks in anticipation of high rewards. An example of this would be investing in new, unproven technology with a view of being "first in the market" in anticipation of highly profitable sales. In this case, it is possible that the technology may not work, and the market may not accept the new product; alternatively, the product may be highly successful and profitable.

While a program or a project is concerned, for the most part, with risks and issues that arise inside the specific program or project, portfolios are concerned with (1) maximizing financial value of the portfolio, (2) tailoring the fit of the portfolio to the organizational strategy and objectives, and (3) determining how to balance the programs and projects within the portfolio given the organization's capacities and capabilities. The objectives of Portfolio Risk Management are to increase the probability and impact of positive events and to decrease the probability and impact of events adverse to the value, the strategic fitness of the portfolio, and the balance of the portfolio.

Potential risk conditions include aspects of an organization's environment that may contribute to portfolio risk, such as poor management practices (a negative risk), integrated management systems (positive), an excessive number of concurrent projects (negative), or dependency on external participants who are highly specialized (positive). Because of the downstream impact on programs and projects, risk management becomes critical for root cause correction of negative risks or capitalization of positive risks at the organizational and at the portfolio level. Investment in risk management that addresses root cause correction generally generates the best return. For example, the investment in quality management—a positive risk—has been demonstrated to be more cost effective in comparison to corrective actions required because of poor quality—a negative risk.

Portfolio Risk Management includes providing reserves (or contingencies) across the threat pool within the component programs and projects. The portfolio manager is in a position to hold an aggregate contingency to cover threats where the expected monetary value is an unreliable guide to contingencies due to a less than statistically significant number of risks within an individual initiative—typically threats with high impact and low probability. A portfolio manager may also aggregate risk responses by using some common characteristic; otherwise the nature of a portfolio is a collection of initiatives only coincidentally coupled and not joined by outcome (i.e., impact or consequence of the opportunity). In other words, there isn't a portfolio risk management element—it is a contingency provision for the constituent projects and programs in cases where each component cannot economically fund protection from threats. This is called equity protection and is commonly used by insurance companies. The opportunity at the equity protection level is the consideration of why an initiative was sanctioned to be in the portfolio in the first place.

While Portfolio Risk Management is embedded in all of the portfolio management processes, there are three key elements in Portfolio Risk Management: risk planning, risk assessment, and risk response. These elements are shown in Figure 8-2. The Portfolio Risk Management processes are:

8.1 Develop Portfolio Risk Management Plan—Planning risk management, including the identification of portfolio risks, portfolio risk owners, risk tolerance, and the creation of risk management processes.

8.2 Manage Portfolio Risks—Executing the portfolio risk management plan, including assessing, responding to, and monitoring risks.

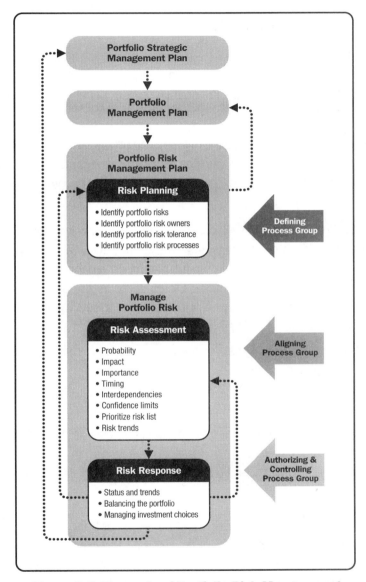

Figure 8-2. Elements of Portfolio Risk Management

Risks that were identified in the Portfolio Risk Planning as part of the Defining Process Group may arise from either external or internal sources as follows:

- **External risk.** Sources include competitors, the competitive market, the financial market, political events, legal requirements, natural events, technological advances, environmental concerns, regulatory requirements, and globalization pressures.

- **Internal risk.** Sources include potential risk sources within the organization where the portfolio resides, such as management decisions, bankruptcy, corruption, lack of integrity, shifting priorities, funding reallocation, and corporate/organizational realignments.

To identify risks related to external competitors, significant amounts of data are captured and investigated through benchmark analysis. Organizational data is compared against peers and best-in-class performers, and the variances are translated into threat and opportunity areas.

Other internal risk conditions may include those aspects of an organization's environment that contribute to portfolio risk, such as poor management practices (a negative risk), integrated management systems (a positive risk), an excessive number of concurrent projects (a negative risk), or dependency on external participants whose training is highly specialized (either a positive or negative risk).

Portfolio management risks may be identified by anyone in an organization including executive management, operations management, the portfolio manager, and the program management team. Each organizational level or portfolio component team has a slightly different perspective of the portfolio's risk and the influences can differ:

- *For executive management,* risk concerns generally involve portfolio value, time to market, and funding and investment measures. These may include customer brand and organization reputation, organizational operating model, impact on organizational strategy and objectives, and existing products and services that will be impacted by the portfolio. Executives will often focus on safeguarding shareholders' investment, company assets, detecting and preventing fraud, and identifying and managing liabilities.

- *For operations management,* risk concerns generally involve issues with product and project development, organization products, services, and processes needed to support change.

- *For the portfolio manager,* risk concerns generally involve reporting, data accuracy, portfolio component risk information availability, the quality of portfolio data, the risks that threaten the link between organizational strategy and the portfolio, as well as those risk concerns of the executive and operations management.

- *For program and project teams,* risk concerns are centered on the portfolio components' time, cost, and scope commitments.

Risk concerns common to all organizational levels are the issues of transparency, organizational integrity, and corruption. Risk sources may potentially be structural or based on the execution of the portfolio or components. In the same way that overall project risks are more than just the sum of individual project risks, portfolio risks are more than just the sum of the portfolio component risks.

- *Structural risks* are those risks concerned with an organization's ability to organize its portfolio mission with the organization's hierarchical and clustered structures, which define the methods and approaches in which the organization operates and performs its tasks. The quality of the organization's portfolio management is also a factor for structural risk; governance and application of best practices may provide opportunities for improvement, whereas overambitious plans, as well as inconsistent or rapidly changing strategy, may present threats to success.

- *Execution risks* are concerned with an organization's ability to coordinate and supervise throughout the accomplishment of its mission, which defines how change is managed in performing the organization's tasks. Managing change includes the interactions between component risks that can lead to the emergence of one or more overall risks. A special set of tools may be used to evaluate the overall effect of interlinked component risks on strategic objectives.

The threshold or attitude of the organization towards the positive or negative effects of risks on the organization's portfolio is called risk tolerance. A risk-tolerant organization is willing to take more risks, such as moving more quickly into new markets, expanding products more quickly, or investing more heavily in new product development. The goals of Portfolio Risk Management are to increase the probability and impact of positive events and to decrease the probability and impact of events adverse to the portfolio. This positive or negative effect may impact not only the portfolio of programs and projects, but also the existing services, products, forecasted results, and benefits which the programs and projects generate; the organization itself; the customers which the organization serves; and market leadership.

Particular resource commitments may need to be at the organizational level because internal risks are wider than the portfolio level. The efficient use of resources for both positive and negative external risks could involve the transfer of risk ownership to an external party. As an example, contractual obligations common in the aircraft industry require subcontractors to comply with voluntary ISO quality management standards. Another example is when a portfolio manager requires a contracting organization to use certified project managers. In addition, requiring contractors or subcontractors to carry various insurances is an example of managing a negative external risk.

8.1 Develop Portfolio Risk Management Plan

A risk management plan is a component of the project, program, or portfolio management plan that describes how risk management activities will be structured and performed. It also includes reference to the corporate risk management guidelines, policies, and procedures that define the organization's risk strategy, tolerance, and thresholds for the organization. The risk management plan provides the approach that will be used by the governing bodies for assessing risk in proposed new portfolio components.

Different types of new investments will be considered knowing that generally venture or growth-type investments carry more attraction due to a higher potential return, but they are a higher organizational stretch and, on average, carry higher risk. In order to maximize return on investment of resources, some high-risk investments may be considered, but the risk management plan will show how the governing bodies should work to balance investment risk and manage the overall expected return against known risks. The result is risk-based decision making.

Figure 8-3 shows the inputs, tools and techniques, and outputs. Figure 8-4 shows the data flow diagram.

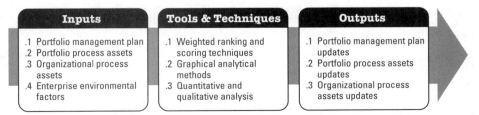

Inputs	Tools & Techniques	Outputs
.1 Portfolio management plan	.1 Weighted ranking and scoring techniques	.1 Portfolio management plan updates
.2 Portfolio process assets	.2 Graphical analytical methods	.2 Portfolio process assets updates
.3 Organizational process assets	.3 Quantitative and qualitative analysis	.3 Organizational process assets updates
.4 Enterprise environmental factors		

Figure 8-3. Develop Portfolio Risk Management Plan: Inputs, Tools and Techniques, and Outputs

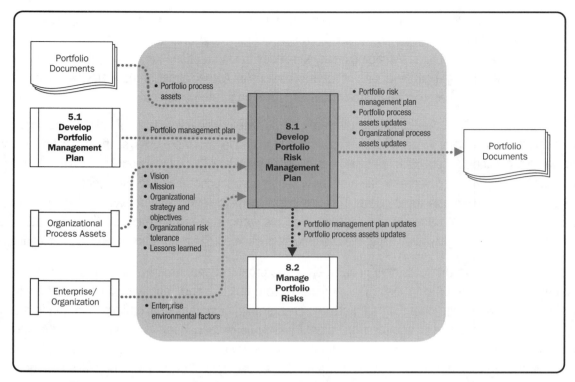

Figure 8-4. Develop Portfolio Risk Management Plan: Data Flow Diagram

8.1.1 Develop Portfolio Risk Management Plan: Inputs

8.1.1.1 Portfolio Management Plan Updates

The portfolio management plan provides guidance regarding governance model, performance management, communication, and stakeholder engagement for developing the risk management plan. It may also define roles and responsibilities for conducting risk management, budgets, risk management activities schedule, risk categories, definition of probability and impact, and stakeholder risk tolerances.

8.1.1.2 Portfolio Process Assets

Relevant portfolio process assets used as input to planning for risk management include, but are not limited to:

- List of portfolio components,
- Portfolio component selection criteria,
- Prioritization algorithms,
- Portfolio risk register,
- Portfolio issue register,
- Portfolio performance matrices,

- Portfolio resources, and
- Portfolio budget.

Information from prior portfolio risks may be available as historic files, actual data, and lessons learned.

8.1.1.3 Organizational Process Assets

In the portfolio risk management plan, organizational portfolio assets required for analysis include, but are not limited to:

- Vision and mission statements,
- Organizational strategy and objectives,
- Organizational risk tolerance, and
- Lessons learned.

8.1.1.4 Enterprise Environmental Factors

Enterprise environmental factors that can affect the risk management plan include organization culture and structure, infrastructure, OPM, legal and regulatory considerations, industry requirements, and market conditions. Published information, including commercial databases, academic studies, market research, and benchmarking may also provide relevant information for the portfolio risk management plan.

8.1.2 Develop Portfolio Risk Management Plan: Tools and Techniques

8.1.2.1 Weighted Rankings and Scoring Techniques

Weighted ranking and scoring techniques may be used by the portfolio manager and governance boards to assess the risks in multiple portfolios and the overall structure of the portfolios (see 5.2.2.3 for an example). Such rankings and scoring are applied to any technical and management risk details during this process. The ranking or scoring is provided by any group or individual with specialized knowledge or training and is available from many sources. It should be noted that the processes for identifying and managing risks are embedded in the Portfolio Management Process Groups and are not necessarily separate activities. Planning identifies areas around risk management, which include, but are not limited to:

- Portfolio risks important to the organization,
- Risk owners,
- Risk tolerance, and
- Risk processes.

High-level plans for conducting the risk management activities are defined by ranking and scoring. Risk management cost elements and schedule activities are developed for inclusion in the portfolio component's budget and schedule, respectively. Risk contingency reserve application approaches may be established or reviewed. Risk management responsibilities are assigned. General organizational templates for risk categories and definitions of terms, such as levels of risk, probability by type of risk, impact by type of objectives, and the probability and impact matrix are tailored to the specific project. If templates for other steps in the process do not exist, they may be generated in these meetings. The outputs of these activities will be summarized in the risk management plan.

8.1.2.2 Graphical Analytical Methods

During the planning processes, the specific tools and models that will be used to measure risk are defined. These tools include, but are not limited to probability (likelihood) and impact (consequences). Although assigning a probability/likelihood rating and an impact/consequences rating are not an exact science, the probability and impact matrix in Figure 8-5 allows a standard view and assessment of the organizational risks.

Probability	Threats					Opportunities				
0.90	0.05	0.09	0.18	0.36	0.72	0.72	0.36	0.18	0.09	0.05
0.70	0.04	0.07	0.14	0.28	0.56	0.56	0.28	0.14	0.07	0.04
0.50	0.03	0.05	0.10	0.20	0.40	0.40	0.20	0.10	0.05	0.03
0.30	0.02	0.03	0.06	0.12	0.24	0.24	0.12	0.06	0.03	0.02
0.10	0.01	0.01	0.02	0.04	0.08	0.08	0.04	0.02	0.01	0.01
	0.05	0.10	0.20	0.40	0.80	0.80	0.40	0.20	0.10	0.05

Impact (ratio scale) on an objective (e.g., cost, time, scope, or quality)

■ = High ☐ = Moderate ▨ = Low

Note: Each risk is rated on its probability of occurring and impact on an objective if it does occur. The organization's thresholds for low, moderate, or high risks are shown in the matrix and determine whether the risk is scored as high, moderate, or low for that objective.

Figure 8-5. Probability and Impact Matrix

Risk probability assessments determine the likelihood for occurrence of each specific risk. Risk impact assessment investigates the potential effect, both negative effects for threats and positive effects for opportunities, on one or more of the portfolio's objectives.

Probability and impact are assessed for each identified risk. Risks may be assessed in interviews or meetings with participants who have been selected because of their familiarity with the risk categories being discussed. Portfolio manager members and knowledgeable persons from outside the portfolio are included. Expert judgment is required because there may not be adequate information on risks from the organization's database of past portfolios, programs, and projects.

The level of probability for each risk and its impact on each objective is evaluated during the interview or meeting. Explanatory details, including assumptions that justify the levels assigned, are also recorded. Risk probabilities and impacts are rated according to the definitions given in the risk management plan. Sometimes risks with obviously low ratings of probability and impact are not retained for additional work but are included in a general category for monitoring (a "watch list").

- *Importance* defines which types or categories are more important than others.

- *Timing* defines when certain risks or types of risks have more impact.

- *Interdependencies* deal with the connections between risks and the connections between types of risks.

- *Confidence limits* define the assurance levels of the risk and performance measures.

- *Prioritize risk lists* defines how risks will be listed and prioritized in a portfolio list.

In addition, tools and techniques are further discussed in Section 4 on Portfolio Performance Management and Section 5 on Portfolio Governance Management.

8.1.2.3 Quantitative and Qualitative Analysis

During the planning processes, there are specific tools and processes, which are identified for analyzing trends, balancing the portfolio, and managing investment choices. These tools and processes include, but are not limited to:

- Status and trend analysis compares current performance data and recent trends, and compares recent changes in the portfolio.

- Rebalancing methods are used to reallocate the portfolio in cases where it has deviated away from the strategy or in order to better balance risk.

- Investment choice tools include the following: (1) trade-off analysis determines the effect of changing one or more factors of the portfolio; (2) market-payoff variability focuses on pricing and sales forecasts and depends on a number of marketing factors, whereby the effects of changing one or more of these factors may affect portfolio itself or the portfolio strategy; (3) budget variability determines the effect of changing the portfolio; (4) performance variability analyzes the performance of the portfolio; (5) market requirement variability analyzes changes in market requirements in relation to the portfolio; and (6) time-to-market variability determines the effects of portfolio velocity.

- Portfolio risk exposure charts provide the following information:

  o *Outcome probability analysis of the portfolio.* The portfolio manager makes estimates of potential portfolio outcomes with respect to the success criteria, listing the possible values of the corresponding performance indicators with their associated confidence levels. This output is typically expressed as a cumulative cost distribution (see Figure 8-6) that the portfolio component manager can use to set realistic targets in line with stakeholder risk tolerances.

  o *Probability of achieving portfolio objectives.* The portfolio manager may estimate the probability of achieving specific objectives under the current plan using modeling techniques as explained previously. Figure 8-6 shows the cumulative frequency of meeting certain cost objectives. For example, in this chart, the portfolio is only 12% likely to meet the $41K target. For 75% likelihood, a forecast of $50K is required.

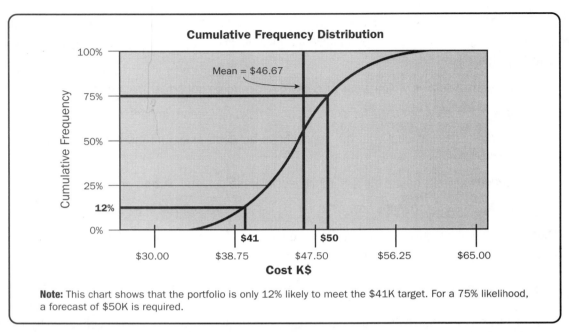

Figure 8-6. Cumulative Cost Chart for the Spend on the Portfolio over a Given Period

8.1.3   Develop Portfolio Risk Management Plan: Outputs

8.1.3.1   Portfolio Management Plan Updates

The portfolio risk management plan updates standard criteria to allow the portfolio team to assess the risks that are identified in an effective fashion consistent with the organizational risk strategy. The portfolio risk management plan details the manner in which risks will be identified and analyzed and how these risk responses will be developed, managed, and communicated. Risk management is an ongoing process and not a single event. The processes, cadence, and reporting are detailed in the portfolio risk management plan.

The portfolio risk management plan describes how risk management is structured and performed in the portfolio. It is a subsidiary plan of the portfolio management plan and includes the following:

- **Methodology.** Defines the approaches, tools, and data sources that may be used to perform risk management on the portfolio.

- **Roles and responsibilities.** Defines the owners, lead, support, and team members for each type of activity in the risk management plan, and clarifies their responsibilities.

- **Risk measures.** Defines the risk categories and criteria for probability and impact, the structure of probability and impact matrix, and the stakeholders' risk tolerances and appetite for risk.

- **Frequency.** Defines when and how often the risk management process will be performed throughout the portfolio cycle, establishes protocols for governance requirements, and establishes risk management activities to be included in the portfolio management plan.

- **Risk categories.** Provides a structure that ensures a comprehensive process of systematically identifying risks to a consistent level of detail and contributes to the effectiveness and quality of the

Identify Risks process. An organization can use a previously prepared categorization framework which may take the form of a simple list of categories. Some categories of risks are shown in Figure 8-7.

Sample Risk Categories
Portfolio component risk
Organizational risk
Performance risk
Resource risk
Financial/budget risk
Market risk
Regulatory risk
Image and public relations risk

Figure 8-7. Risk Categories

There a number of ways to plan for portfolio risks. Organizations identify different risks based on the needs of the organization and the categories of risks described in the introduction to this section. These may include the types of risks shown in Figure 8-7 and may arise from a number of situations specific to the management of portfolios:

8.1.3.2   Portfolio Process Assets Updates

Development of the portfolio risk management plan may lead to the update of portfolio process assets, such as portfolio funding.

8.1.3.3   Organizational Process Assets Updates

The portfolio manager may have recommendations for the update of organizational process assets, such as risk checklists, new risk categories, or subcategories.

8.2 Manage Portfolio Risks

Manage Portfolio Risks consists of four stages: (1) risks are identified, (2) risks are analyzed, (3) risk responses are developed, and (4) risks are monitored and controlled throughout the Manage Portfolio Risk process. Figure 8-8 shows the inputs, tools and techniques, and outputs. Figure 8-9 shows the data flow diagram.

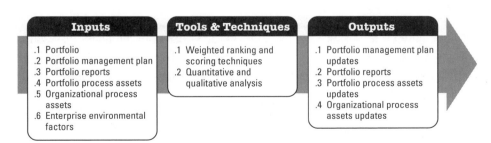

Inputs	Tools & Techniques	Outputs
.1 Portfolio	.1 Weighted ranking and scoring techniques	.1 Portfolio management plan updates
.2 Portfolio management plan	.2 Quantitative and qualitative analysis	.2 Portfolio reports
.3 Portfolio reports		.3 Portfolio process assets updates
.4 Portfolio process assets		.4 Organizational process assets updates
.5 Organizational process assets		
.6 Enterprise environmental factors		

Figure 8-8. Manage Risks: Inputs, Tools and Techniques, and Outputs

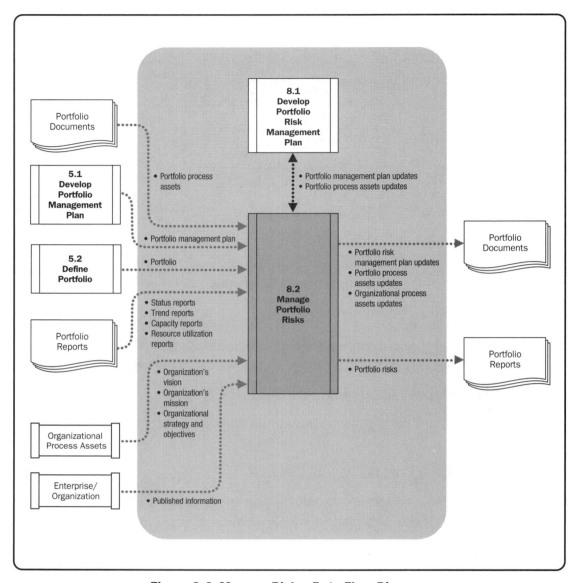

Figure 8-9. Manage Risks: Data Flow Diagram

8.2.1 Manage Portfolio Risks: Inputs

8.2.1.1 Portfolio

The portfolio includes authorized portfolio components. Portfolio risks are identified for each of the authorized portfolio components, as well as for risk events that may affect more than one program or project. Portfolio component dependencies such as logical, logistical, and benefits realization dependencies are also mapped analyzing the portfolio.

As a part of the portfolio, the portfolio risks and portfolio issues are managed as follows:

- **Portfolio Risk Register.** Portfolio risks are documented in a risk register. The development of the risk register begins with Develop Portfolio Risk Management Plan. The risk register ultimately contains the outcomes of the Manage Portfolio Risks process. The information in the risk register will subsequently be used and updated by portfolio management and portfolio risk management processes. The risk register contains the following information:

- *List of identified risks.* The identified negative risks, including their root causes and assumptions, are documented. This includes the recognition of positive risks to explore how to increase the chances of realizing opportunities.

- *Risk owner.* The portfolio manager designates a person accountable for effective management of the corresponding risk. This person's role is to ensure analysis and, as necessary, to assign response-related actions, and to monitor the situation for as long as the risk is current.

- *List of potential responses.* Potential responses to a risk may be identified during the risk identification process.

- *Probability Impact Assessment.* Risk probabilities and impacts are rated according to the definitions given in the portfolio risk management plan.

- *Risk triggers.* These are the fundamental conditions or events that may give rise to the identified risk.

- *Updated risk categories.* The process of identifying risks can lead to new risk categories being added. The risk breakdown structure (RBS), if documented in the portfolio management plan, may need to be enhanced or amended based on the outcomes.

- **Portfolio Issues.** In contrast to portfolio risks, issues are events that have a current impact on the portfolio. If negative risks are not identified and treated—they become issues. If positive risk are not identified and treated—they become missed opportunities. It is also useful to track and document portfolio issues using an issues register or list.

8.2.1.2 Portfolio Management Plan

Identifying portfolio risks requires an understanding of the portfolio roadmap, funding, and some technical knowledge about the portfolio components involved. In particular, the portfolio risk management plan provides structure and guidance for performing portfolio risk identification, including roles and responsibilities, guidelines on use of tools, and details of the time and budget allocated to portfolio risk management.

8.2.1.3 Portfolio Reports

Portfolio reports include, but are not limited to, performance reports, governance decision reports, status reports, trend reports, capacity reports, resource utilization (and capacity) reports, funding/budget reports and strategic alignment reports. Portfolio reporting includes some consolidated perspective on portfolio component status and performance. Portfolio reports, in general, and portfolio performance reports, specifically, are important indicators for managing risks. Performance of a portfolio may introduce new risks while mitigation of risks could lead to better performance. Reports are traditional or in the form of dashboard reporting.

8.2.1.4 Portfolio Process Assets

Portfolio process assets include any or all process-related assets, from any or all of the stakeholders and teams involved in the portfolio, which can be used to influence the portfolio's success and risk posture. The portfolio process assets also include the portfolio-related knowledge bases, such as lessons learned and historical information, which may help in managing risks. Templates used for risk management may also prove to be helpful.

8.2.1.5 Organizational Process Assets

Organizational process assets (OPAs), such as the organization's vision and mission, strategy and objectives, and values, may be used.

8.2.1.6 Enterprise Environmental Factors

Published information, including commercial databases, academic studies, benchmarking, or other industry studies, may be useful in identifying risks.

8.2.2 Manage Portfolio Risks: Tools and Techniques

8.2.2.1 Weighted Ranking and Scoring Techniques

As a part of the Authorizing and Controlling Process Group, the governing board uses weighted ranking and scoring techniques during recurring governance meetings to evaluate the existing risks and identify whether any new risks have arisen (see an example in 5.2.2.3). These techniques may be used in meetings dedicated to reviewing risks or those where the review of key risks is an agenda item but not necessarily the overall purpose of the meeting, for example, executive governance meetings, organizational strategy meetings, or investment meetings, etc.

8.2.2.2 Quantitative and Qualitative Analysis

In order to manage the portfolio risks, the portfolio manager may use a number of quantitative and qualitative tools to better understand the interdependencies, importance, timing, and confidence limits. These tools can perform sensitivity and trade off analysis, modeling and simulation (e.g. "what if scenarios") and determine variability and trends in schedule, budget, performance, and time-to-market. Variance and trend analysis using performance data from the portfolio components may be reviewed on a regular basis to determine deviations from the baseline, which may indicate the potential impact of threats or opportunities. Trends are also useful for evaluating the effectiveness of earlier risk response actions.

Once all portfolio performance, risk, and governance information is gathered and reviewed, the governance board can begin to assess the portfolio and consider rebalancing portfolio components, resource requirements, and portfolio budget in order to realign the portfolio risks.

- **Quantitative analysis.** Quantitative tools are generally used to measure financial metrics. Financial metrics include but are not limited to the following: net present value (NPV)—a measure of a series of cash flows; estimated net present value (ENPV)—a measure of future NPVs; payback or payback period (PBP)—a measure of the time required for a return on investment; return on investment (ROI)—a measure of the efficiency of an investment; and internal rate of return (IRR)—the discount rate used in budgeting, which makes the NPV equal to zero.

- **Sensitivity analysis.** Sensitivity analysis helps to determine which risks have the most potential impact on the portfolio. It examines the extent to which the uncertainty of each element affects the respective objective when all other uncertain elements are held at their baseline values. One typical output of sensitivity analysis is the tornado diagram; this is useful for displaying which parameters lead to a high degree of variability and which have less effect (see Figure 8-10).

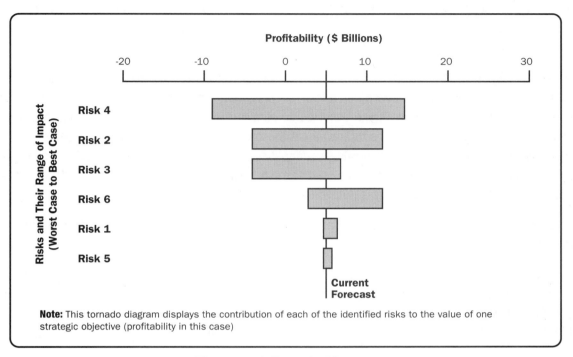

Figure 8-10. Tornado Diagram

- **Modeling and simulation.** Simulation uses a model that translates the uncertainties specified at a detailed level of the portfolio into their potential combined impact on portfolio objectives. Simulations are typically performed using the Monte Carlo technique. In a simulation, the model is computed many times (iterated). At each iteration, the input values (such as cost of project elements or duration of schedule activities) are randomized in accordance with the probability distribution of the corresponding variable. The outputs of each iteration are consolidated to provide a frequency distribution for the values of each key parameter (such as total cost or completion date).

- **Qualitative analysis.** Qualitative tools are generally used to provide a way to measure domains of portfolio risks that are not specifically quantitative. These may include risk probability and impact assessment, sensitivity analysis, modeling and simulation, assumptions analysis, influence diagrams, risk-portfolio component chart, weighted ranking and scoring techniques, heat maps, and ranking and scoring of portfolio risks.

- **Investment choice analysis.** Investment choice pertains to the alignment of the portfolio. This analysis focuses on the new and changing strategic objectives/goals and indicates where there are gaps in investment within the portfolio as a whole. Gaps may constitute portfolio risks.

The variance analysis process compares the planned results to the actual results. Outcomes from this analysis may forecast any potential deviation from the baseline plan at project completion. Deviation from the baseline plan may indicate the potential impact of threats or opportunities.

Performance review measurements compare and analyze the objectives in quantifiable measurements which may be used to compare the actual results with the target. This helps to forecast the degree of success in achieving the portfolio scope.

There are two types of risk: external and internal. Several risk response strategies can be considered for each risk. The portfolio manager, along with the risk owner, should select the strategy or mix of strategies most likely to be effective. The risk owner should make decisions to choose the most appropriate response strategy or mix of strategies and develop specific actions to implement those decisions. The risk owner may select primary and alternative strategies. The risk owner may develop contingency plans and identify the conditions which trigger their execution. Often a contingency reserve is allocated for time or cost. Finally, the risk owner may develop a fallback plan for execution if the selected strategy is not sufficiently effective.

Strategies may include: response strategy selection, strategies for both threats and opportunities, and scenario analysis.

Once a set of actions, based on the selected strategies, has been defined, the potential result of these actions is assessed with respect to the success criteria of the portfolio. This analysis may entail repeating the processes for identifying and analyzing the portfolio risks. It also entails modifying the existing plans, when necessary, in order to ensure that the response actions become an integral part of the portfolio plan.

8.2.3 Manage Portfolio Risks: Outputs

8.2.3.1 Portfolio Management Plan Updates

Updates to the portfolio management plan and its subsidiary plans may be necessary once the risk response plans are accepted, for example, the portfolio budget may have to be increased to cover preventive actions or to allow for contingency reserves, schedule, and resources. To ensure that the agreed-upon actions are implemented and monitored as part of ongoing portfolio management, the portfolio management plan is updated as response activities are formally approved.

8.2.3.2 Portfolio Reports

Portfolio reports include the top portfolio risks in the risk register after all risk analysis is completed and adjustments have been made. It may be beneficial to develop a grouping of risks by category and by component using a risk component chart (see Figure 8-11).

Risk ID	Component 1			Component 2			Component 3			Etc.		
	S	C	O	S	C	O	S	C	O	S	C	O
	Structural Risks											
R1	★			★			★					
	Component Risks											
R2		★										
R3		★										
R4		★			★							
R5								★				
	Overall Risks											
R6			★			★						
R7			★						★			
Etc.												

Note: Structural Risk R1 affects three components (Component 1, Component 2, and Component 3); Risk R4 appears in two components (Component 1 and Component 2), which suggests that there may be a common cause; Risk R6 arises from the combined effect from Components 1 and 2.

Figure 8-11. Risk Component Chart

Portfolio reports include portfolio issues in the issue register after analysis is completed for those risks that were realized and includes the response actions that will be taken.

Governance recommendations are also part of portfolio reports and include portfolio risk status and responses. Action plans are developed and updates are then communicated to the portfolio governing body. Recommendations may include new risks, new status, new responses or new actions planned, or recommendations for changes to portfolio components based on risks. Examples of changes recommended to portfolio components include: a recommended increase in funding, a change in staff allocated to address a risk with expected high impact to the portfolio, new portfolio components, portfolio components to be terminated, or portfolio components to be changed.

The process of managing risks produces various portfolio reports, including risk responses and analysis. These reports are updates to the overall portfolio reports.

8.2.3.3 Portfolio Process Asset Updates

Managing risks will cause updates to the portfolio risk register, the portfolio issues register, and other documents. If governance recommendations for changes to portfolio components based on risks are accepted, then portfolio component lists will need to be updated as well.

8.2.3.4 Organizational Process Asset Updates

Organizational process assets, such as the risk assessment for the organization, may be updated as a result of portfolio risk management.

ANNEX A1

THE STANDARD FOR PORTFOLIO MANAGEMENT

A1.1 Introduction

Portfolio management is a set of interrelated, strategic organizational management processes that facilitate informed and objective decision making regarding investments of time, money, and other resources in work intended to achieve strategic goals. The portfolio components and management processes are selected to produce specific benefits to the organization; therefore, selecting portfolio management processes is a strategic decision.

A1.2 What is a Standard?

The PMI standards program defines a standard as: "A document approved by a recognized body, which provides for common and repeated use, rules, guidelines, or characteristics for products, processes, or services with which compliance is not mandatory."

This standard identifies that subset of project portfolio management generally recognized as good practice.

A1.3 The Framework for this Standard

This standard describes the key elements of portfolio management. This standard is not prescriptive in nature and therefore does not specify the means by which an organization should implement the portfolio management processes described herein. This standard presumes that the organization has an organizational strategy accompanied by mission and vision statements as well as strategic goals and objectives. In order to implement the portfolio processes presented here, the following conditions are needed:

- The organization—including executive management—embraces the practice of portfolio management;
- Proposed projects and programs need to be evaluated;
- Appropriately skilled staff members are available to manage the portfolio;
- Project management processes exist;
- The organizational roles and responsibilities are defined; and
- Mechanisms are in place to communicate organization decisions throughout the organization.

Figure A1-1 illustrates the relationships among the Portfolio Management Process Groups. Figure A1-1 shows that these groups have interdependencies and the portfolio manager utilizes these Process Groups in

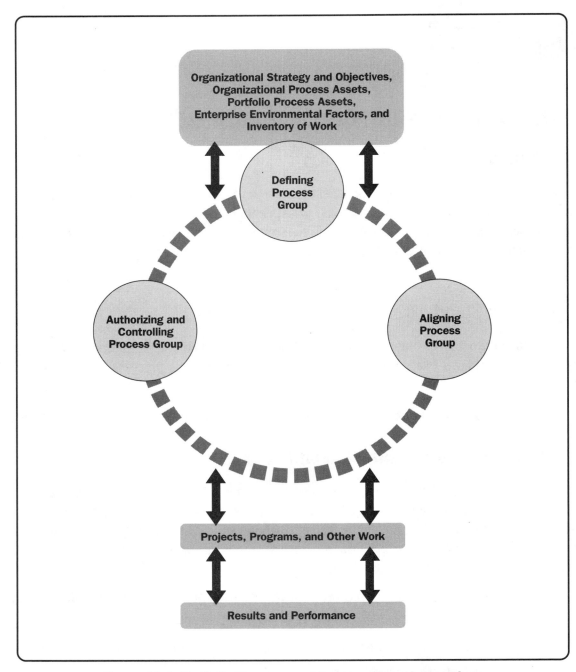

Figure A1-1. Portfolio Management Process Group Interactions

the management of each portfolio. Constituent processes may also interact, both within their particular Process Group and with the other Portfolio Management Process Groups. The three Portfolio Management Process Groups are:

- **Defining Process Group.** Determines how strategic objectives will be implemented in a portfolio and defines and authorizes a portfolio or subportfolio; develops the portfolio management plan.

- **Aligning Process Group.** Determines how portfolio components will be categorized, evaluated, selected for inclusion, and managed in the portfolio.

- **Authorizing and Controlling Process Group.** Determines how to monitor strategic changes; tracks and reviews performance indicators for alignment; and authorizes the portfolio and verifies values that are delivered to the organization from the portfolio.

The portfolio manager often repeats these group and individual constituent processes during the portfolio management process. The Process Groups are not phases, and do not constitute a life cycle. The Process Groups may be repeated for each portfolio or subportfolio.

The remainder of this section provides information and interlinks processes shown in Figure A1-1 for establishing and managing portfolio components, details the Process Groups, and includes the following major sections:

A1.4 Portfolio Management Process Groups

A1.5 Defining Process Group

A1.6 Aligning Process Group

A1.7 Monitoring and Controlling Process Group

A1.4 Portfolio Management Process Groups

The following sections identify and describe the Portfolio Management Process Groups. These Process Groups have clear dependencies and are typically performed in the same sequence for each portfolio. They are independent of application areas or industry focus. The portfolio manager may repeat individual Process Groups and individual constituent processes prior to portfolio component authorization.

Table A1-1 reflects the mapping of the 16 portfolio management processes into the three Portfolio Management Process Groups and the five Portfolio Management Knowledge Areas. Each of the key portfolio management processes is shown in the Process Group in which most of the activity takes place.

Table A1-1. Portfolio Management Process Groups and Knowledge Areas Mapping

Knowledge Areas	Process Groups		
	Defining Process Group	Aligning Process Group	Authorizing and Controlling Process Group
Portfolio Strategic Management	4.1 Develop Portfolio Strategic Plan 4.2 Develop Portfolio Charter 4.3 Define Portfolio Roadmap	4.4 Manage Strategic Change	
Portfolio Governance Management	5.1 Develop Portfolio Management Plan 5.2 Define Portfolio	5.3 Optimize Portfolio	5.4 Authorize Portfolio 5.5 Provide Portfolio Oversight
Portfolio Performance Management	6.1 Develop Portfolio Performance Management Plan	6.2 Manage Supply and Demand 6.3 Manage Portfolio Value	
Portfolio Communication Management	7.1 Develop Portfolio Communication Management Plan	7.2 Manage Portfolio Information	
Portfolio Risk Management	8.1 Develop Portfolio Risk Management Plan	8.2 Manage Portfolio Risks	

The process flow diagram shown in Figure A1-2 provides an overall summary of the basic flow and interactions among Process Groups, organizational strategy and objectives, organization process context, and the program and project management processes. A Process Group includes the constituent portfolio management processes that are linked by the respective inputs and outputs, where the result or outcome of one process becomes the input to another. The Process Groups should not be thought of as portfolio management phases.

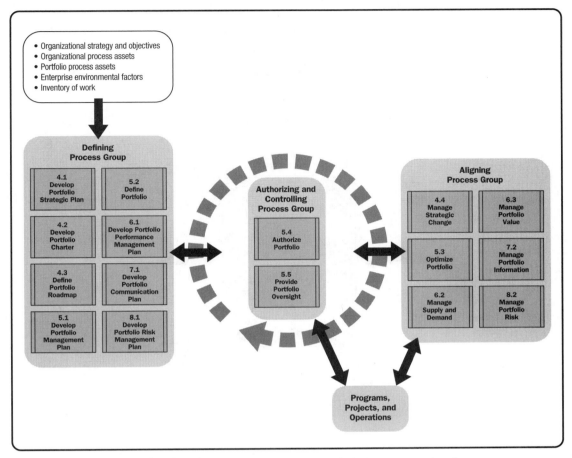

Figure A1-2. Portfolio Management Process Group Interactions

A1.5 Defining Process Group

The Defining Process Group consists of those processes performed to establish how the organizational strategy and objectives will be implemented in a portfolio; determines the portfolio structure and roadmap; defines and authorizes a portfolio or subportfolio; and develops the portfolio management plan and subsidiary plans.

The Defining Process Group illustrated in the center of Figure A1-3 is most active at the time the organization identifies and updates its strategic goals, near-term budgets, and plans. Traditionally, these activities take place at the annual budgeting time although some organizations have more or less frequent cycles. Such activities could be scheduled quarterly, for example, or may occur because of unscheduled changes in the organization climate.

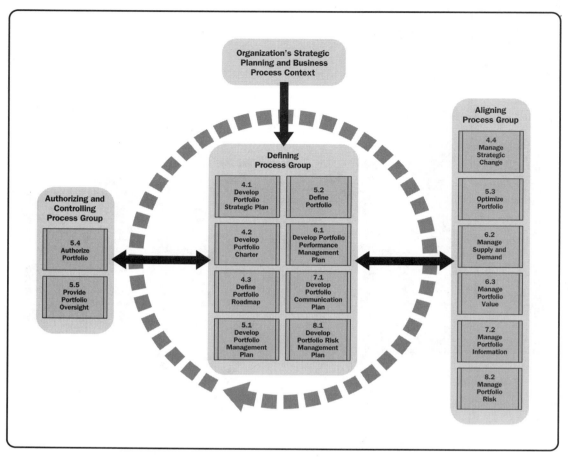

Figure A1-3. Defining Process Group Interactions

A1.5.1 Develop Portfolio Strategic Plan

Develop Portfolio Strategic Plan is the process of evaluating the organization's high-level strategy and objectives and documenting the strategy and objectives relative to the given portfolio to ensure alignment of the organization's and portfolio's strategy and objectives. The portfolio strategic plan includes the vision, goals, objectives, strategies, and other information specific to the portfolio. The portfolio strategic plan is produced and approved by key stakeholders, governing bodies, and portfolio managers. Refer to Figure A1-4 for inputs and outputs.

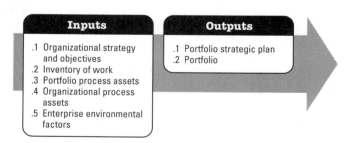

Figure A1-4. Develop Portfolio Strategic Plan: Inputs and Outputs

A1.5.2 Develop Portfolio Charter

Develop Portfolio Charter is the process of defining and documenting the portfolio structure based on strategies and objectives defined in the portfolio strategic plan. The charter authorizes the portfolio manager to apply portfolio resources to portfolio components and to execute the portfolio management processes. The charter also identifies the portfolio and subportfolios included relative to the identified organizational areas defined in the portfolio strategic plan. Refer to Figure A1-5 for inputs and outputs.

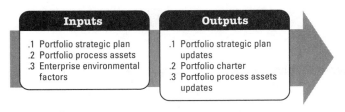

Figure A1-5. Define Portfolio Charter: Inputs and Outputs

A1.5.3 Define Portfolio Roadmap

Define Portfolio Roadmap is an iterative process to document high-level strategic direction and information about the portfolio in a chronological representation. The roadmap portrays the alignment to strategies, dependencies, sequencing, timing, and expected resource requirements of portfolio components in the portfolio. Program roadmaps may be included in the portfolio roadmap. Refer to Figure A1-6 for inputs and outputs.

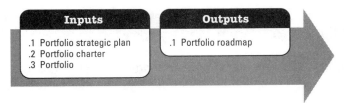

Figure A1-6. Define Portfolio Roadmap: Inputs and Outputs

A1.5.4 Develop Portfolio Management Plan

Develop Portfolio Management Plan is the process of developing, coordinating, and integrating all subsidiary plans into a comprehensive portfolio management plan. This plan also aligns with the portfolio strategic plan, the portfolio charter, and the portfolio roadmap. This plan describes how the portfolio is defined, organized, authorized, and controlled. Refer to Figure A1-7 for inputs and outputs.

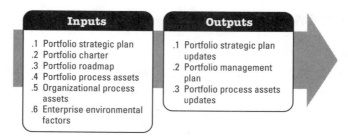

Figure A1-7. Develop Portfolio Management Plan: Inputs and Outputs

A1.5.5 Define Portfolio

Define Portfolio is the process that creates an up-to-date list of qualified portfolio components by identifying, categorizing, scoring, and ranking portfolio components to which a common set of decision filters and criteria can be applied for evaluation, prioritization, balancing, and selection. Refer to Figure A1-8 for inputs and outputs.

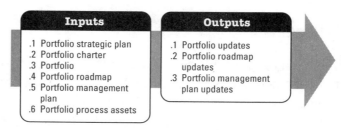

Figure A1-8. Define Portfolio: Inputs and Outputs

A1.5.6 Develop Portfolio Performance Management Plan

Develop Portfolio Performance Management Plan is the process that establishes how resource capacity will be measured against resource utilization and changing demand, how the value realization will be tracked and measured, and how the stakeholders and the portfolio manager will be provided with metrics to monitor portfolio performance. Refer to Figure A1-9 for inputs and outputs.

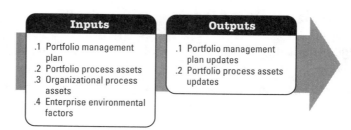

Figure A1-9. Develop Portfolio Performance Management Plan: Inputs and Outputs

A1.5.7 Develop Portfolio Communication Management Plan

Develop Portfolio Communication Management Plan is the process of gathering and analyzing the portfolio stakeholder communication requirements so that an appropriate communication strategy and tactics can be defined, documented, and communicated. Refer to Figure A1-10 for inputs and outputs.

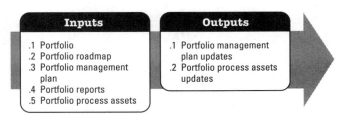

Figure A1-10. Develop Portfolio Communication Management Plan: Inputs and Outputs

A1.5.8 Develop Portfolio Risk Management Plan

Develop Portfolio Risk Management Plan establishes the risk strategy, risk tolerance, and risk thresholds for the organization that enables risk-based decision making with regard to managing the portfolio. Refer to Figure A1-11 for inputs and outputs.

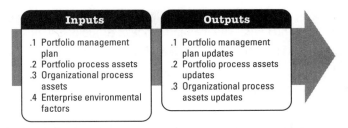

Figure A1-11. Develop Portfolio Risk Management Plan: Inputs and Outputs

A1.6 Aligning Process Group

The Aligning Process Group consists of processes to manage and optimize the portfolio (see Figure A1-12). The Aligning Process Group ensures the availability of information regarding the strategic goals that the portfolio is to support, as well as, operational rules for evaluating components and building the portfolio. The processes in this Process Group help to establish a structured method for aligning the mix of portfolio components to the organization's strategy.

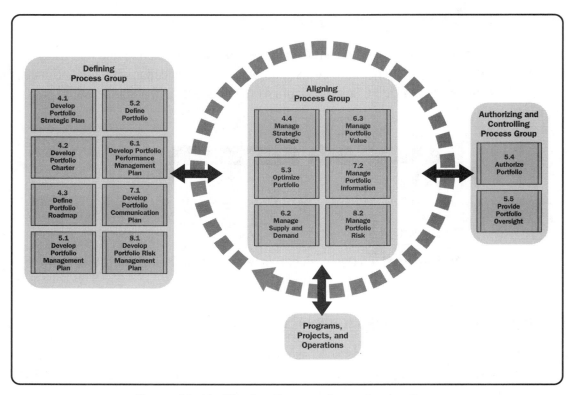

Figure A1-12. Aligning Process Group Interactions

The Aligning Process Group is most active after the portfolio organization has defined and developed its strategic goals, near-term budgets, and plans. The Aligning Process Group is the most active of the Process Groups. Traditionally, these activities are used to manage ongoing portfolio activities.

A1.6.1 Manage Strategic Change

Manage Strategic Change is the process of managing changes to the portfolio, portfolio management planning, or portfolio management structure to ensure continued alignment of the portfolio with the organizational strategy or objectives as they change. Refer to Figure A1-13 for inputs and outputs.

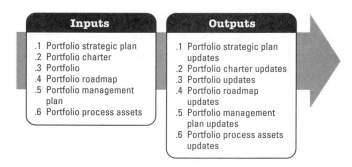

Figure A1-13. Manage Strategic Change: Inputs and Outputs

A1.6.2 Optimize Portfolio

Optimize Portfolio is the process of evaluating the portfolio based on the organization's selection criteria, prioritizing portfolio components, and creating the portfolio component mix that aligns with the organizational strategy and has the greatest potential to achieve the organizational objectives with the available resources. Refer to Figure A1-14 for inputs and outputs.

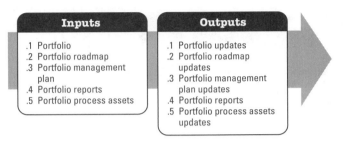

Figure A1-14. Optimize Portfolio: Inputs and Outputs

A1.6.3 Manage Supply and Demand

Manage Supply and Demand is the process of allocating the supply of organizational resources available to the portfolio against the portfolio resource demand, based on organizational priorities and potential value of the portfolio components. Refer to Figure A1-15 for inputs and outputs.

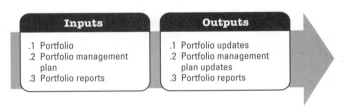

Figure A1-15. Manage Supply and Demand: Inputs and Outputs

A1.6.4 Manage Portfolio Value

Manage Portfolio Value is the process of monitoring the expected value to be delivered by the portfolio components as they are executed and measuring the value delivered to the organization as portfolio components are completed. Refer to Figure A1-16 for inputs and outputs.

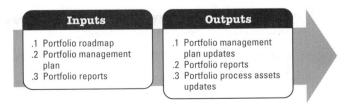

Figure A1-16. Manage Portfolio Value: Inputs and Outputs

A1.6.5 Manage Portfolio Information

Manage Portfolio Information is the process of collecting, analyzing, storing, and delivering required information to portfolio stakeholders according to the portfolio management plan. Portfolio reporting is an output of multiple processes, which represents the wide variety of information that is included. Refer to Figure A1-17 for inputs and outputs.

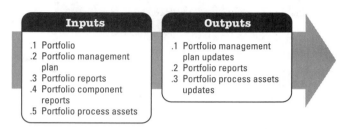

Figure A1-17. Manage Portfolio Information: Inputs and Outputs

A1.6.6 Manage Portfolio Risks

Manage Portfolio Risks is the process of identifying and analyzing portfolio risks, developing responses to the risks, and monitoring and controlling the portfolio risks. Refer to Figure A1-18 for inputs and outputs.

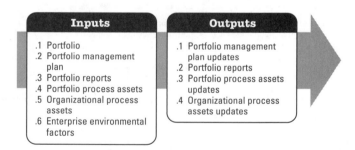

Figure A1-18. Manage Portfolio Risks: Inputs and Outputs

A1.7 Authorizing and Controlling Process Group

The Authorizing and Controlling Process Group consists of the processes for determining how to authorize the portfolio and provides ongoing portfolio oversight. These two processes are central to all the portfolio management processes and are the activities necessary to ensure that the portfolio as a whole is performing to achieve predefined metrics determined by the organization. The authorizing and oversight processes are very active parts of the portfolio and are usually an ongoing function of the organization's governing board (see Figure A1-19).

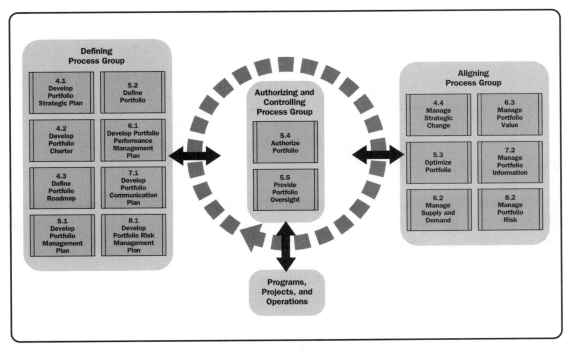

Figure A1-19. Authorizing and Controlling Process Group Interactions

A1.7.1 Authorize Portfolio

Authorize Portfolio is the process of authorizing approved portfolio components for execution, allocating resources to authorized portfolio components, and communicating the portfolio components authorization information. Refer to Figure A1-20 for inputs and outputs.

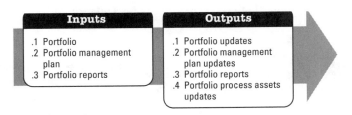

Inputs	Outputs
.1 Portfolio	.1 Portfolio updates
.2 Portfolio management plan	.2 Portfolio management plan updates
.3 Portfolio reports	.3 Portfolio reports
	.4 Portfolio process assets updates

Figure A1-20. Authorize Portfolio: Inputs and Outputs

A1.7.2 Provide Portfolio Oversight

Provide Portfolio Oversight is the process of monitoring the portfolio performance and recommended changes to the portfolio component mix, portfolio component performance, and compliance to organizational standards to understand when changes need to be made to the portfolio or to the portfolio management processes. This process includes execution, documentation, and communication of the decisions and the resulting actions taken. Refer to Figure A1-21 for inputs and outputs.

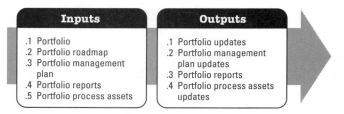

Figure A1-21. Provide Portfolio Oversight: Inputs and Outputs

A1.8 Process Groupings

Portfolio management processes are linked by the respective inputs and outputs, where the result or outcome of one process becomes the input to another. Groupings of inputs and outputs and groupings of tools and techniques are presented in the following subsections.

A1.8.1 Inputs and Outputs Groupings

The inputs and outputs to the portfolio management processes fall into several categories. Many of these items are both inputs and outputs to the same process.

These inputs and outputs fall into four categories:

- **Guiding**—Provides the strategy or high-level direction for the portfolio;
- **Supporting**—Provide processes, tools, and capabilities to facilitate the operation of the portfolio management processes;
- **Planning**—Provides specific direction as to how these processes are executed; and
- **Reporting**—Provides information that is used both within the portfolio team and with stakeholders.

Figure A1-22 shows the alignment of the inputs and outputs for *The Standard for Portfolio Management – Third Edition* to these categories.

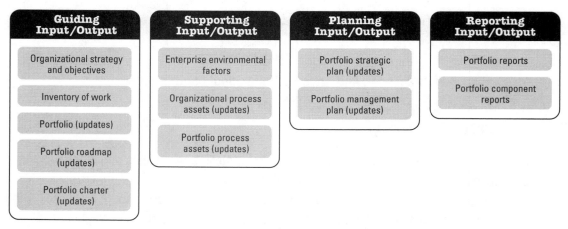

Figure A1-22. Portfolio Management Input/Output Groupings

A1.8.2 Process Tools and Techniques Groupings

Tools and techniques are the methods by which inputs are processed or analyzed to create outputs. The tools and techniques of the portfolio management processes fall into several categories. Many of these tools and techniques are used in more than one process.

These tools and techniques fall into four categories:

- **Analyzing**—Uses tools and techniques to analyze process inputs, resulting in additional information that becomes the process outputs;

- **Selection**—Provides methods to facilitate selection of the appropriate portfolio components;

- **Meeting**—Provides mechanisms to share information and make decisions in a group interaction style; and

- **Information**—Provide methods to obtain or share information relevant to the portfolio.

Figure A1-23 shows the alignment of the tools and techniques to the groupings:

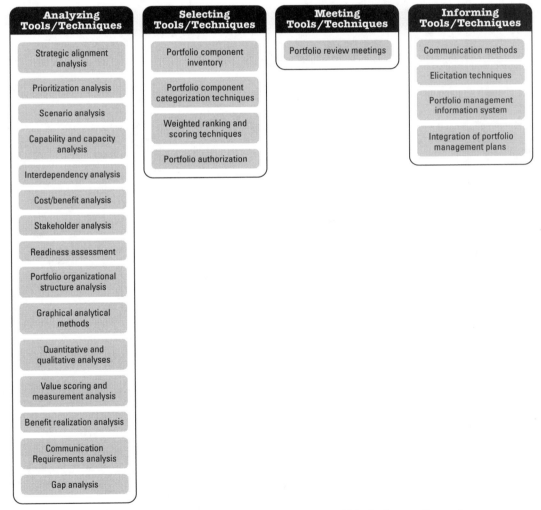

Figure A1-23. Portfolio Management Tools and Techniques Groupings

APPENDIX X1

THIRD EDITION CHANGES

The purpose of this appendix is to give a detailed explanation of the changes made to *The Standard for Portfolio Management* – Second Edition to help readers understand the differences between editions and the rationale for the standard, and to provide historical continuity.

The project committee was chartered to update and enhance *The Standard for Portfolio Management*—Second Edition. The following sources and criteria were used to determine requisite changes to the standard:

- Recommendations deferred from *The Standard for Portfolio Management* – Second Edition;
- Results of a portfolio management market research study that validated proposed changes to *The Standard for Portfolio Management* – Second Edition, including additions and changes to Knowledge Areas and processes;
- Harmonization of key sections and concepts with the PMI foundational standards;
- Recommendations from subject matter expert review;
- Alignment with the *PMI Lexicon of Project Management Terms*;
- Recommendations from public standards program working sessions; and
- Recommendations from public exposure draft comments.

X1.1 Structural Changes

There are key differences in structure. *The Standard for Portfolio Management* – Third Edition is structured to integrate the expansion of Knowledge Areas and Process Groups for Portfolio Management to those in *The Standard for Portfolio Management* – Second Edition, as described in the side-by-side comparison of distinctions in Table X1.1.

X1.1.1 Addition of Knowledge Areas and Process Groups

In *The Standard for Portfolio Management*—Third Edition, three Knowledge Areas have been added which map to three Process Groups. These Knowledge Areas expand on concepts and themes present in *The Standard for Portfolio Management*—Second Edition but not described as processes. Portfolio Strategic Management, Portfolio Performance Management, and Portfolio Communication Management Knowledge Areas have been added to the Portfolio Governance and Portfolio Risk Management Knowledge Areas in *The Standard for Portfolio Management*—Second Edition.

Table X1-1. Structural Changes

2008 Revision	2012 Revision
Section I—The Portfolio Management Framework Chapters 1 and 2	Sections 1 Introduction Section 2 Portfolio Management Overview and Organization

Section II—The Standard for Portfolio Management Chapter 3 Portfolio Management Processes
   Aligning Process Group
   Monitoring and Controlling Process Group
	Section 3 Portfolio Management Process Groups
	   Defining Process Group
	   Aligning Process Group
	   Authorizing and Controlling Process Group

Section III—The Portfolio Management Knowledge Areas Chapters 4 and 5	Section 4 Portfolio Strategic Management Section 5 Portfolio Governance Management Section 6 Portfolio Performance Management Section 7 Portfolio Communication Management Section 8 Portfolio Risk Management
Section IV—Appendices	Annex A1 Appendices X1 and X2
Section V—Glossary and Index	Glossary and Index

In *The Standard for Portfolio Management*—Third Edition, one Process Group was added and one renamed. The Defining Process Group contains key processes to define and plan execution of the portfolio processes. The Monitoring and Controlling Process Group from *The Standard for Portfolio Management*—Second Edition has been renamed to the Authorizing and Controlling Process Group.

X1.1.2 Writing Styles

PMI standards committees use a style guide provided by PMI to create and finalize the content. PMI standards are developed using "active voice" language and are intended to provide consistent content throughout the document. Special attention is paid to uniformity with other PMI standards.

X1.2 Section 1—Introduction Changes

Fundamental changes to the standard are described in Section 1, which has been revised to reflect the standard Knowledge Areas and processes by which portfolio management is widely practiced today. Section 1.1 on Purpose highlights the alignment of this standard with other PMI standards. There is also further discussion on the interactions between project, program, and portfolio management in Section 1, and expansion on the portfolio manager's role, knowledge, and skills and the organizational factors involved in portfolio management. The business value derived from the effective use of portfolio, program, and project management practices is discussed.

Table X1.2 summarizes the changes between editions:

Table X1-2. Section 1 Changes

2008 Revision	2012 Revision
1.1 Purpose of *The Standard for Portfolio Management* 1.1.1 Audience for *The Standard for Portfolio Management*	1 Purpose of *The Standard for Portfolio Management* 1.1.1 Audience for *The Standard for Portfolio Management*
1.2 What is a Portfolio? 1.2.1 The Relationships Among Portfolios, Programs, and Project	1.2 What is a Portfolio?
1.3 What is Portfolio Management?	1.3 What is Portfolio Management?
1.4 The Link between Portfolio Management and Organization Governance	1.4 The Link between Portfolio Management and Organization Governance
1.5 The Relationship between Portfolio Management and Organizational Strategy	1.5 Relationships among Portfolio Management, Program Management, Project Management, and Operations Management 1.5.1 Interactions between Portfolio, Program and Project Management 1.5.2 Program Management 1.5.3 Project Management 1.5.4 Operations Management
1.6 The Relationships Among Portfolio, Program, and Project Management	1.6 Business Value
1.7 The Link between Portfolio Management and Operations Management 1.7.1 The Link between Portfolio Management and Operational Projects 1.7.2 Operational Stakeholders in Portfolio Management	1.7 Role of the Portfolio Manager 1.7.1 Portfolio Manager Knowledge and Skills
1.8 Role of the Portfolio Manager 1.8.1 Strategic Alignment 1.8.2 Portfolio Management Methods and Techniques 1.8.3 Program and Project Management Methods and Techniques 1.8.4 Process Development and Continuous Improvement 1.8.5 General Business Skills 1.8.6 General Management Skills 1.8.7 Stakeholder engagement 1.8.8 Risk and Opportunity Management	1.8 Role of the PMO in Portfolio Management 1.8.1 Portfolio Management Office Functions
1.9 Portfolio Management Reporting and Metrics 1.9.1 Portfolio Reporting and the PMO 1.9.2 Portfolio Management Metrics	1.8 Portfolio Management Body Of Knowledge

X1.3 Section 2—Portfolio Management Overview and Organization

In building a stronger link between portfolio management and other organizational governance processes more detail regarding the relationship between strategic planning and portfolio management was added. Detail regarding the initiation and process improvement of portfolio management processes has been added. More emphasis on the information through the use of a Portfolio Management Information System is included.

Table X1.3 summarizes the changes between the editions:

Table X1-3. Section 2 Changes

2008 Revision	2012 Revision
2.1 Portfolio Management Process Overview 2.1.1 Strategy and Investment Alignment 2.1.2 Portfolio Component Management Life Cycle 2.1.3 Portfolio Management Process Cycle 2.1.4 Establishing a Portfolio Management Process	2.1 Introduction
2.2 Portfolio Stakeholder Roles and Responsibilities 2.2.1 Executive Review Board 2.2.2 Portfolio Process Group 2.2.3 Portfolio Management Board 2.2.4 Portfolio Managers 2.2.5 Sponsors 2.2.6 Program Managers 2.2.7 Project Managers 2.2.8 Program/Project Management Office 2.2.9 Project Team 2.2.10 Marketing Management 2.2.11 Operations Management 2.2.12 Engineering Management 2.2.13 Legal Management 2.2.14 Human Resource Management 2.2.15 Functional Managers 2.2.16 Finance Managers 2.2.17 Customers 2.2.18 Vendors/Business Partners	2.2 Portfolio Management and Organizational Strategy and Objectives
2.3 Organizational Influences 2.3.1 Organizational Culture 2.3.2 Economic Impact 2.3.3 Organizational Impacts 2.3.4 Enterprise Environmental Factors	2.3 Establishing a Portfolio Management Process 2.3.1 Assessment of Organizational Maturity and Strategic Fit 2.3.2 Portfolio Management Initiation 2.3.3 Portfolio Management Setup 2.3.4 Portfolio Management Continuous Improvement
	2.4 Portfolio Management Process Cycle
	2.5 Portfolio Management Information System (PMIS)
	2.6 Portfolio Management Governance
	2.7 Portfolio Stakeholders

X1.4 Section 3—Portfolio Management Processes

Section 3 has been revised to map to the Knowledge Areas being introduced in *The Standard for Portfolio Management* – Third Edition. Section 3 serves as a standard for managing a portfolio and clearly indicates the five required Portfolio Management Process Groups and their constituent processes. Some of the processes were combined to provide consistent granularity of detail. Processes were added to capture concepts in Sections 1 and 2 in *The Standard for Portfolio Management* – Second Edition.

Table X1.4 summarizes the changes between the editions:

Table X1-4. Section 3 Changes

2008 Revision	2012 Revision
3.1 Portfolio Management Process Interactions	3.1 Portfolio Management Process Interactions 3.1.1 Common Inputs and Outputs 3.1.1.1 Portfolio Process Assets 3.1.1.2 Portfolio Reports 3.1.1.3 Portfolio governance recommendations and decisions 3.1.1.4 Organizational Process Assets 3.1.1.5 Enterprise Environmental Factors
3.2 Portfolio Management Process Groups	3.2 Portfolio Management Process Groups
	3.3 Defining Process Group 3.3.1 Develop Portfolio Strategic Plan 3.3.2 Develop Portfolio Charter 3.3.3 Define Portfolio Roadmap 3.3.4 Develop Portfolio Management Plan 3.3.5 Define Portfolio 3.3.6 Develop Portfolio Performance Management Plan 3.3.7 Develop Portfolio Communication Plan 3.3.8 Develop Portfolio Risk Management Plan
3.3 Aligning Process Group 3.3.1 Identify Components 3.3.2 Categorize Components 3.3.3 Evaluate Components 3.3.4 Select Components 3.3.5 Identify Portfolio Risks 3.3.6 Analyze Portfolio Risks 3.3.7 Prioritize Components 3.3.8 Develop Portfolio Risk Responses 3.3.9 Balance Portfolio 3.3.10 Communicate Portfolio Adjustment 3.3.11 Authorize Components	3.4 Aligning Process Group 3.4.1 Manage Strategic Change 3.4.2 Optimize Portfolio 3.4.3 Manage Supply and Demand 3.4.4 Manage Portfolio Value 3.4.5 Manage Portfolio Information 3.4.6 Manage Portfolio Risks
3.4 Monitoring and Controlling Process Group 3.4.1 Monitor and Control Portfolio Risks 3.4.2 Review and Report Portfolio Performance 3.4.3 Monitor Business Strategy Changes	3.5 Authorizing and Controlling Process Group 3.5.1 Authorize Portfolio 3.5.2 Provide Portfolio Oversight

X1.5 Sections 4 through 8 Changes

Content for the previous Chapters 4 and 5 have been expanded to Sections 4 through 8. Three new Knowledge Areas have been added and expanded upon, including inputs, tools and techniques, and outputs for each of these areas of portfolio management knowledge. New processes have been added to include concepts in previous editions that were not in processes. Processes from *The Standard for Portfolio Management* – Second Edition have been mapped to the five Knowledge Areas *The Standard for Portfolio Management* – Third Edition. The Knowledge Areas in *The Standard for Portfolio Management* – Third Edition are:

X1.5.1 Section 4 Portfolio Strategic Management

X1.5.2 Section 5 Portfolio Governance Management

X1.5.3 Section 6 Portfolio Performance Management

X1.5.4 Section 7 Portfolio Communication Management

X1.5.3 Section 8 Portfolio Risk Management

Tables X1.5 through X1.9 summarize the changes between the chapter contents of the editions:

Table X1-5. Section 4 Portfolio Strategic Management Changes

2008 Revision	2012 Revision
4.1 Identify Components	4.1 Develop Portfolio strategic plan
4.2 Categorize Components	4.2 Develop Portfolio Charter
4.3 Evaluate Components	4.3 Define Portfolio Roadmap
4.4 Select Components	4.4 Manage Strategic Change
4.5 Prioritize Components	
4.6 Balance Portfolio	
4.7 Communicate Portfolio Adjustment	
4.8 Authorize Components	
4.9 Review and Report Portfolio Performance	
4.10 Monitor Business Strategy Changes	

Table X1-6. Section 5 Portfolio Governance Management Changes

2008 Revision	2012 Revision
5.1 Identify Portfolio Risks	5.1 Develop Portfolio Management Plan
5.2 Analyze Portfolio Risks	5.2 Define Portfolio
5.3 Develop Portfolio Risk Responses	5.3 Optimize Portfolio
5.4 Monitor and Control Portfolio Risks	5.4 Authorize Portfolio
	5.5 Provide Portfolio Oversight

Table X1-7. Section 6 Portfolio Performance Management Changes

2008 Revision	2012 Revision
	6.1 Develop Portfolio Performance Management Plan 6.2 Manage Supply and Demand 6.3 Manage Portfolio Value

Table X1-8. Section 7 Portfolio Communication Management Changes

2008 Revision	2012 Revision
	7.1 Develop Portfolio Communication Plan 7.2 Manage Portfolio Information

Table X1-9. Section 8 Portfolio Risk Management Changes

2008 Revision	2012 Revision
	8.1 Develop Portfolio Risk Management Plan 8.2 Manage Portfolio Risks

X1.5 Sections 4 through 8 Process Mapping

Tables X1.10 through X1.14 map the processes between the editions:

Table X1-10. Section 4 Portfolio Strategic Management Mapping

2008 Revision	2012 Revision
4.10 Monitor Business Strategy Changes	4.1 Develop Portfolio Strategic Plan 4.2 Develop Portfolio Charter 4.3 Define Portfolio Roadmap 4.4 Manage Strategic Change

Table X1-11. Section 5 Portfolio Governance Management Mapping

2008 Revision	2012 Revision
4.1 Identify Components 4.2 Categorize Component 4.3 Evaluate Components 4.4 Select Components 4.5 Prioritize Components 4.6 Balance Portfolio 4.8 Authorize Components	5.1 Develop Portfolio Management Plan 5.2 Define Portfolio 5.3 Optimize Portfolio 5.4 Authorize Portfolio 5.5 Provide Portfolio Oversight

Table X1-12. Section 6 Portfolio Performance Management Mapping

2008 Revision	2012 Revision
	6.1 Develop Portfolio Performance Management Plan
	6.2 Manage Supply and Demand
	6.3 Manage Portfolio Value

Table X1-13. Section 7 Portfolio Communication Management Mapping

2008 Revision	2012 Revision
4.7 Communicate Portfolio Adjustment	7.1 Develop Portfolio Communication Plan
4.9 Review and Report Portfolio Performance	7.2 Manage Portfolio Information

Table X1-14. Chapter 8 Portfolio Risk Management Mapping

2008 Revision	2012 Revision
5.1 Identify Portfolio Risks	8.1 Develop Portfolio Risk Management Plan
5.2 Analyze Portfolio Risks	8.2 Manage Portfolio Risks
5.3 Develop Portfolio Risk Responses	
5.4 Monitor and Control Portfolio Risks	

X1.6 Glossary

The glossary has been expanded and updated to:

- Include those terms within *The Standard for Portfolio Management* – Third Edition that need to be defined to support an understanding of the standard's contents;

- Clarify meaning and improve the quality and accuracy of any translations;

- Eliminate terms not used within *The Standard for Portfolio Management* – Third Edition; and

- Ensure alignment with the *PMI Lexicon of Project Management Terms*.

APPENDIX X2

CONTRIBUTORS AND REVIEWERS OF *THE STANDARD FOR PORTFOLIO MANAGEMENT* – THIRD EDITION

The Project Management Institute is grateful to all of these individuals for their support and acknowledges their outstanding contributions to the project management profession.

X2.1 *The Standard for Portfolio Management* – Third Edition Core Committee

The following individuals served as leaders in the development of the standard and were major contributors of text and concepts.

Jen L. Skrabak, PMP, MBA, Chair
Michael Reed, PMP, Vice Chair
M. Elaine Lazar, MA, AStd, PMI Project Specialist
Karl (Andy) Anderson, PMP
Steve Butler, MBA, PMP
Clive Enoch, PMP
Yvan Petit, PhD, PMP
Gwen Whitman, PMP
Wende Wiles, PMP, RMP

X2.2 Subcommittee Members

In addition to the members of the Committee, the following individuals provided input to drafts of the standard:

Sangeeta Agarwal, Msc (Tech), PMP
Panagiotis Agrapidis, MSc, C.Eng
Shyamprakash K. Agrawal, PMP, PgMP
Rhonda L. Arrington, PMP, MPH
Vahid Azadmanesh, PMP, RMP
Subashish Bose, PMP
Alison B. Bushon, PMP
Cynthia D. Casebolt, PMP
Pius Anton Christopher, PMP, CITP
Amrita Datta, MBA, PMP

Kenn Dolan, PMP

Bob Dombroski, PMP

Steve Emokpaire, CEng, PMP

AliReza Farhoodi, MSc, PMP

Michael D. Farley, MBA, PMP

Andreas Fellner, MS, PMP

Ralf Finchett, Jr., MAPM, BSc (hons)

Serge Goncharov, PMP, PgMP

Susan Taguiam Huang, MPM, PMP

Brian Irwin, MSM, PMP

Samir Mathur, PMP

Jennifer Mazon

Kiran Mundy

Craig Norgard, PMP, ITIL v3 Expert

Jason Papadopoulos, MBCS, CITP

Francesca Pratt, PMP

Rob Reader, PMP

Krupakara Reddy, PMP, PRINCE2

Guy Schleffer, PMP, PgMP

Jenine Serviolo, PMP, SDI Facilitator

Clare J. Settle, PMP

Venkat K. Sharma, PMP, PgMP

Mei Jing Subrina Shih, PMP, CPIM

Thierry Verlynde, PMP, MSc

Susan Weese

Kyle S. Wills, PgMP, PMP

X2.3 Significant Contributors

Farhad Abdollahyan, PMP, OPM3 Certified Professional

Dorothy L. Kangas, PMP

Carol Steuer, PMP

X2.4 Reviewers

X2.4.1 SME Review

Norberto Almeida

Lalonde Benoît, PMP, OPM3

Iain Fraser, PMP, PMI Fellow

Jim Peters

X2.4.2 MAG Review

Monique Aubry, PhD, MPM
Chris Cartwright, MPM, PMP
Laurence Goldsmith, MBA, PMP
Paul E. Shaltry, PMP
Cyndi Snyder, MBA, PMP, EVP

X2.4.3 Consensus Body Review

Monique Aubry, PhD, MPM
Nigel Blampied, PE, PMP
Dennis L. Bolles, PMP
Peggy J. Brady
Chris Cartwright, MPM, PMP
Sergio Coronado
Andrea Demaria
Charles T. Follin, PMP
Laurence Goldsmith, MBA, PMP
Dana J Goulston, PMP
Dorothy L. Kangas, PMP
Thomas Kurihara
Timothy MacFadyen
David Christopher Miles, CEng, OPM3-CC
Mike Musial, PMP, CBM
Deborah O'Bray, CIM, PMI Fellow
Nanette Patton, MSBA, PMP
Crispin ("Kik") Piney, BS, PgMP
Paul E. Shaltry, PMP
Geree V. Streun, PMP, PMI-ACP
Matthew D Tomlinson, PMP, PgMP
Dave Violette, MPM, PMP

X2.4.4 Exposure Draft Review

Ahmad Khairiri Abdul Ghani, MBA, Int. PE
Homam Al khateeb, PMP, PMI-RMP
José Rafael Alcalá Gómez, PMP, MBA
Haluk Altunel, PhD, PMP
Vijaya Chandar Avula, PMP, CSQA
Ammar N. Baidas, PMP, PgMP
Manuel F. Baquero V., MSc, PMP

Harwinder Singh Bhatia, PMP, CSM
Peter Bigelow
Lynda Bourne, DPM, PMP
Damiano Bragantini
Fabio Luiz Braggio, PMP, MBA
Kevin Brennan, PMP, CBAP
James F Carilli, MBA, PgMP
Marcin Chomicz, MBA, PMP
Kris De Ridder, PMP
Maria Angela de Souza Fernandes
Carlos Eustáquio Soukef Domingos, PMP, MsC
Sheila Donohue, MBA, PMP
R. Bernadine Douglas, MS, PMP
Fam Woon Fong, PMP, PMI-RMP
Diego Alfonso Flórez Torres, PMP
Charles T. Follin, PMP
Taralyn Rose Frasqueri-Molina, PMP, CAPM
Emerson Ricardo Furlaneto
Jose Eduardo Motta Garcia, MBA, PMP
Ivo Gerber, PMI-SP, OPM3
Alcides Gimenes, PMP
Theofanis Giotis
Herb Goergen, PMP, P.Eng.
Aditya Gokhale
Gary Hamilton, MBA, PgMP
Nurani Vinod Hariharan, CISA
Michael K. Harris
Simon Harris, PMP, Prince2
Walter Hekala, PMP, CQA
Hisashi Hirose
Keith D. Hornbacher, MBA
Shuichi Ikeda
Rajesh Jadhav, PMP, PgMP
Ashok Jain, PMP, CSM
Tony Johnson, PMP, PgMP
Yves Jordan, PMP
Adil J. Khan, PMP, PMI-RMP
Henry Kondo, PMP, CISA
Richard P. Krulis, PMP
Thomas M. Kurihara
Sébastien Kurtz, MBA, PMP

Ginger Levin, PMP, PgMP

John Louis, PMP, BSc (Hon)

Juan Verastegui Maldonado, MBA, PMP

Richard Maltzman, PMP

Gary Marx

Paul Mehlberg, PMP

Vijo Menon

Carlos Morais, MSc, PMP

Kevin R. Morrison, MBA, PMP

Venkateswar P. Oruganti, PMP, FIETE FIE

Crispin ("Kik") Piney, BSc, PgMP

Jose Angelo Pinto, PMP, OPM3 CC

Joshua R. Poulson, PMP, PMI-ACP

Dana L. Purvis, PMP

Vijay Reddy

Alexander Revin, PMP

Bernard Roduit

Bradley Rogers

Koroush Sanaeimovahed, PMP

Hemant Seigell, MBA, PMP

Cindy Shelton

Mauro Sotille

Shoji Tajima, PMP, ITIL

Biagio Tramontana, PMP

Doreen True, PMP

Michelle Turner

Dipak Varshney

Basskar Verma

Aloysio Vianna Jr. PMP, M.Eng.

Reinhard Wagner, CPM, PPMC

Tim Washington

Patrick Weaver, PMP, PMI-SP

Kevin Wegryn

Rebecca A. Winston, JD

X2.5 PMI Standards Program Member Advisory Group (MAG)

The following individuals served as members of the PMI Standards Program Member Advisory Group during development of the standard:

Monique Aubry, PhD, MPM

Margareth F.S. Carneiro, MSc, PMP

Chris Cartwright, MPM, PMP
Terry Cooke-Davies, PhD
Laurence Goldsmith, MBA, PMP
Paul E. Shaltry, PMP
Cyndi Snyder, MBA, PMP, EVP
John Zlockie, MBA, PMP, PMI Standards Manager

X2.6 Production Staff

Special mention is due to the following employees of PMI:

Donn Greenberg, Publications Manager
Roberta Storer, Product Editor
Barbara Walsh, Publications Planner

X2.7 Harmonization Team

Steve Butler, MBA, PMP
Folake Dosunmu, PgMP, OPM3
Dorothy L. Kangas, PMP
Joseph W. Kestel, PMP
Timothy MacFadyen
Vanina Mangano
David Christopher Miles, CEng, OPM3-CC
Eric S. Norman, PMP, PgMP
Michael Reed, PMP
Chris Richards, PMP
Jen L. Skrabak, MBA, PMP
Carol Steuer, PMP
Bobbye S. Underwood, PMP, PMI-ACP
Dave Violette, MPM, PMP

X2.8 Harmonization Team: PMI Staff

Randy Holt, MBA, PMP, Chair
Karl F. Best, CAPM, CStd
M. Elaine Lazar, MA, AStd
Kristin Vitello, CAPM
Quynh Woodward, MBA, PMP
John Zlockie, MBA, PMP

X2.9 Contributors to Past Editions

X2.9.1 *The Standard for Portfolio Management* (2006)

X2.9.1.1 Core Team

David W. Ross, PgMP, PMP, Project Manager
Paul E. Shaltry, PMP, Deputy Project Manager
Kristin L. Vitello, CAPM, PMI Project Specialist
Claude Emond, MBA, PMP
Laurence Goldsmith, MBA, PMP
Nancy Hildebrand, BSc, PMP
Jerry Manas, PMP

Patricia G. Mulcair, PMP
Beth Ouellette, PMP
Tom E. Vanderheiden, PMP
Clarese Walker, PMP
David Whelbourn, MBA, PMP
Michael A. Yinger

X2.9.1.2 Other Contributors:

Mohamed Hosney Abdelgelil
Fred Abrams, PMP, CPL
Pankaj Agrawal, PMP, CISA
Eduardo O. Aguilo, PMP
Zubair Ahmed, PMP
Mounir A. Ajam, MS, PMP
Hussain Ali Al-Ansari, Eur Ing, C Eng.
Jose Correia Alberto, MSc, LCGI
Mohammed Abdulla Al-Kuwari, C Eng., PMP
Greg Alexander, PhD, PE
Joyce Alexander
Petya Alexandrova, PMP
Shelley M. Alton, MBA, PMP
Luis E. Alvarez Dionisi, MS, PMP
Neelu Amber
Cynthia Anderson, PMP
Ronald L. Anderson, MPM, PMP
Mauricio Andrade, PMP
Jayant Aphale, PhD, MBA
Michael Appleton, CMC, PMP
V. Alberto Araujo, MBA, PMP
Jose Carlos Arce Rioboo, PMP
Alexey O. Arefiev, PMP
Mario Arlt, PMP
Julie Arnold, PMP

Canan Z. Aydemir
Darwyn S. Azzinaro, PMP
AC Fred Baker, MBA, PMP
Rod Baker, MAPM, CPM
Lorie A. Ballbach, PMP
Harold Wayne Balsinger
Keith E. Bandt, PMP
Kate Bankston, PMP
Anil Bansal
Christina Barbosa, PMP
Mohammed Safi Batley, MIM
John P. Benfield, PMP
Randy Bennett, PMP, RCC
A. Kent Bettisworth
David D. Bigness, Jr.
Susan S. Bivins, PMP
Dennis L. Bolles, PMP
Jeroen Bolluijt
Dave M. Bond, PhD, PMP
Stephen F. Bonk, PMP, PE
Herbert Borchardt, PMP
Ann Abigail Bosacker, PMP
Christine M. Boudreau
Laurent Bour, PMP
Lynda Bourne, DPM, PMP
Mark E. Bouska, PMP
Sonia Boutari, PMP

David Bradford, PMP
Peggy J. Brady, PMP
Adrienne L. Bransky, PMP
Donna Brighton, PMP
Shirley F. Buchanan, PMP
JoAnn Bujarski
Matthew Burrows, MIMC, PMP
Jacques Cantin
James D. Carlin, PMP
Margareth F. Santos Carneiro, MsC, PMP
Brian R. Carter, PMP
Jose M. Carvalho, PMP
Pietro Casanova, PMP
Trevor Chappell, FIEE, PMP
Gordon Chastain
Deepak Chauhan, APM, PMP
Eshan S. Chawla, MBA, PMP
Keith Chiavetta
Jaikumar R. Chinnakonda, PMP
Edmond Choi
Sandra Ciccolallo
Rachel A. Ciliberti, PMP
Lisa Clark
Kurt J. Clemente Sr., PMP
Kathleen M. Clore, PMP
Aaron Coffman, PMP

John E. Cormier, PMP
April M. Cox, PMP
Mark R. Cox, PMP
Margery J. Cruise, MSc, PMP
Wanda Curlee, PMP
Nancy A. Cygan, PMP
Damyan Georgiev Damyanov
Kiran M. Dasgupta, MBA, PMP
Sushovan Datta
Kenneth M. Daugherty, PMP
Stephanie E. Dawson, PMP
Pallab K. Deb, MBA, B Tech
Nikunj Desai
D. James Dickson, PMP
Christopher DiFilippo, PMP
Peter Dimov, CBM, PMP
Vivek Dixit
Janet Dixon, EdD, PMP
Ross Domnik, PMP
Anna Dopico, PMP
Jim C. Dotson, PMP
Karthik Duddala
Renee De Mond
Karen K. Dunlap, PMP, SSGB
Charles A. Dutton, PMP
Jeffrey J. Dworkin, PMP
Lowell D. Dye, PMP
Barbara S. Ebner
Daniella Eilers
Michael G. Elliott
Michael T. Enea, PMP, CISSP
Michael P. Ervick, MBA, PMP
Clifton D. Fauntroy
Linda A. Fernandez, MBA
Ezequiel Ferraz, PMP
Maviese A. Fisher, IMBA, PMP
Joyce M. Flavin, PMP
Jacqueline Flores, PMP
Robert J. Forster, MCPM, PMP
Carolyn A. Francis, PMP
Serena E. Frank, PMP

Kenneth Fung, MBA, PMP
Stanislaw Gasik
Lorie Gibbons, PMP
Lisa Ann Giles, PMP
John Glander
Sunil Kumar Goel, PMP
Victor Edward Gomes, BSc, PMP
Andres H. Gonzalez D. ChE
Mike Goodman, PMP, MSEE
Ferdousi J. Gramling
Alicia Maria Granados
Bjoern Greiff, PMP
Steve Gress, PMP
Naveen Grover
Yvonne D. Grymes
Claude L. Guertin, BSc, PMP
Papiya Gupta
Bulent E. Guzel, PMP
Michael F. Hanford
Deng Hao
Cheryl Harris-Barney
Mohamed Hefny
Holly Hickman
Robert Hierholtz, PMP, MBA
David A. Hillson, PhD, PMP
Kenji Hiraishi, PMP
MD Hudon, PMP
Sandy Yiu Fai Hui
Charles L. Hunt
Harold S. Hunt, PMP
Zeeshan Idrees, BSc
Isao Indo, PMP, PE, JP
Andrea Innocenti, PMP
Suhail Iqbal, PE, PMP
Anshoom Jain, PMP
Venkata Rao Jammi, MBA, PMP
David B. Janda
Haydar Jawad, PMP
Grant Jefferson, PMP
G. Lynne Jeffries, PMP
Monique Jn-Marie, PMP

Kenneth L. Jones, Jr., PMP
Martin H. Kaerner, Dr-Ing
Craig L. Kalsa, PMP
Kenday Samuel Kamara
Michael Kamel, PEng, PMP
Malle Kancherla, PMP
Soundaian Kamalakannan
Saravanan Nanjan Kannan, PMP
Barbara Karten, PMP
Ashish Kemkar, PMP
Geoffrey L. Kent, PMP
Todd M. Kent, PMP
Thomas C. Keuten, PMP, CMC
Sandeep Khanna, MBA, PMP
Karu Godwin Kirijath
Raymond R. Klosek, PMP
Richard M. Knaster, PMP
Mary M. Kosovich, PE, PMP
Victoria Kosuda
Sudeendra Koushik, PMP
Narayan Krish, MS, PMP
S V R Madhu Kumar, MBA, PMP
Polisetty Veera Subrahmanya
   Kumar, PMP
Puneet Kumar
Girish Kurwalkar, PMP
Janet Kuster, MBA, PMP
Puneet Kuthiala, PMP
Olaronke Arike Ladipo, MD
Guilherme Ponce de Leon S. Lago,
   PMP
Robert LaRoche, PMP
David W. Larsen, PMP
Terry Laughlin, PMP
Fernando Ledesma, PM, MBA
Ade Lewandowski
Corazon B. Lewis, PMP
Jeffrey M. Lewman, PMP
Lynne C. Limpert, PMP
Giri V. Lingamarla, PMP
Cheryl D. Logan, PMP

J. Kendall Lott, PMP

Dinah Lucre

Angela Lummel, PMP

Susan MacAndrew, MBA, PMP

Douglas Mackey, PMP

Saji Madapat, PMP, CSSMBB

Erica Dawn Main

Subbaraya N. Mandya, PMP

Ammar W. Mango, PMP, CSSBB

Tony Maramara

Hal Markowitz

Franck L. Marle, PhD, PMP

Sandeep Mathur, MPD, PMP

Glen Maxfield, MBA, PMP

Dean R. Mayer

Warren V. Mayo, PMP, CSSBB

Philippe Mayrand, PMP

Yves Mboda, PMP

Amy McCarthy

Richard C. McClarty, Sr.

Eric McCleaf, PMP

Russell McDowell, M Eng, PMP

Malcolm McFarlane

Graham McHardy

Christopher F. McLoon

Kevin Patrick McNalley, PMP

David McPeters, PMP

Carl J. McPhail, PMP

Vladimir I. Melnik, MSc, PMP

Philip R. Mileham

Laura L. Miller, PMP

M. Aslam Mirza, MBA, PMP

Rahul Mishra

Nahid Mohammadi, MS

Sandhya Mohanraj, PMP

Subrata Mondal

Donald James Moore

Balu Moothedath

Roy E. Morgan, PE, PMP

Sharon D. Morgan-Redmond, PMP

Saradhi Motamarri, MTech, PMP

Ralf Muller, PMP

Seetharam Mukkavilli, PhD, PMP

Praveen Chand Mullacherry, PMP

Kannan Sami Nadar, PMP

Sreenikumar G. Nair

Vinod B. Nair, MBA. B Tech

Carlos Roberto Naranjo, PMP

Kazuhiko Okubo, PE, PMP

Nigel Oliveira, BBA, PMP

Sean O'Neill, PMP

Bradford Orcutt, PMP

Rolf A. Oswald, PMP

Louis R. Pack, PMP

Sukanta Kumar Padhi, PMP

Lennox A. Parkins, MBA, PMP

Anil Peer, PEng, PMP

Sameer K. Penakalapati, PMP

Robert E. Perrine, PMP, ITIL-SM

Zafeiris K. Petalas PhD Candidate

Susan Philipose

Crispin (Kik) Piney, PMP

D. Michele Pitman

Charles M. Poplos, EdD, PMP

Todd Porter

Ranganath Prabhu, PMP

Mitch Provost, PMP

Yves Pszenica, PMP

Sridhar Pydah, PMP

Peter Quinnell, MBA

Sueli S. Rabaca, PMP

Madhubala Rajagopal, MCA, PMP

Mahalingam Ramamoorthi, PMP

Sameer S. Ramchandani, PMP

Prem G. Ranganath, PMP, CSQE

Raju N. Rao, PMP, SCPM

Tony Raymond, PMP

Carolyn S. Reid, MBA, PMP

Geoff Reiss, FAPM, MPhil

Bill Rini, PMP

Steven F. Ritter, PMP

Cynthia Roberts

Andrew C. Robison, PMP

Allan S. Rodger, PMP

Bernard Roduit

Randy T. Rohovit

Dennis M. Rose, PMP

Jackson Rovina, PMP

Julie Rundgren

Diana Russo, PMP

Gunes Sahillioglu, MSc, MAPM

Banmeet Kaur Saluja, PMP

Mansi A. Sanap

Nandakumar Sankaran

Kulasekaran C. Satagopan, PMP, CQM

Chandrashekar Satyanarayana, PMP

Margaret H.M. Schaeken, PMP, BSc Math (Hon)

Gary Scherling, PMP, ITIL

John Schmitt, PMP

Neils (Chris) Schmitt

Mark N. Scott

Stephen F. Seay, PMP

Sunita Sekhar, PMP

David Seto, PMP

Clare J. Settle, PMP

Nandan Shah, PMP

Marty Sheets, MBA, PMP

Shoukat M. Sheikh

Kazuo Shimizu, PMP

Donna- Mae Shyduik

Larry Sieck

Derry Simmel, PMP, MBA

Arun Singh, PMP, CSQA

Deepak Singh, PMP

Anand Sinha

Ron Sklaver, PMP, CISA

Michael I. Slansky, PMP

Nancy A. Slater, MBA, PMP

Christopher Sloan

X2

Dennis M. Smith

Noel Smyth

Jamie B. Solak, MAEd

Keith J. Spacek

Gomathy Srinivasan, PMP

Srinivasan Govindarajulu, PMP

Joyce Statz, PhD, PMP

Marie Sterling, PMP

Leigh M. Stewart, MBA, PMP

Martin B. Stivers, PMP

Curtis A. Stock, PMP

Michael E. Stockwell

Sander Stoffels

LeConte F. Stover, MBA, PMP

Anthony P. Strande

Juergen Sturany, PMP

Kalayani Subramanyan, PMP

Mohammed Suheel, BE, MCP

George Sukumar

Patricia Sullivan-Taylor, MPA, PMP

Vijay Suryanarayana, PMP

Dawn C. Sutherland, PMP

Alexander M. Tait

Masanori Takahashi, PMP

Martin D. Talbott, PMP

Ali Taleb, MBA, PMP

David E. Taylor, PMP

Sai K. Thallam, PMP

Ignatius Thomas, PMP

James M. Toney, Jr.

Eugenio R. Tonin, PMP

Jonathan Topp

Massimo Torre, PhD, PMP

Murthy TS, PMP

Shi-Ja Sophie Tseng, PMP

Yen K. Tu

Ian Turnbull

Dr. M. Ulagaraj, PhD

Srikanth U.S MS, PMP

Marianne Utendorf, PMP

Nageswaran Vaidyanathan, PMP

Ernest C. Valle, MB., PMP

Thierry Vanden Broeck, PMP

Gary van Eck, PMP

Paula Ximena Varas, PMP

Jayadeep A. Vijayan, B Tech, MBA

Alberto Villa, MBA, PMP

Dave Violette, MPM, PMP

Ludmila Volkovich

Namita Wadhwa, CAPM

Thomas Walenta, PMP

Jane B. Walton, CPA

Yongjiang Wang, PMP

Michael Jeffrey Watson

Patrick Weaver, PMP, FAICD

Kevin R. Wegryn, MA, PMP

Richard A. Weller, PMP

Thomas Williamson, PMP

Rebecca A. Winston, JD

Ian M.C. Wolfe, MPM, PMP

Rick Woods, MBA, PMP

Fan Wu

Cai Ding Zheng, PMP

Yuchen Zhu, PMP

Leon Zilber, MSc, PMP

X2.9.2 *The Standard for Portfolio Management* – Second Edition (2008)

X2.9.2.1   Core Team

Laurence Goldsmith, MBA, PMP, Project Manager

Maria J. Hondros, MBA, PMP, Deputy Project Manager

M. Elaine Lazar, MA, AStd, PMI Project Specialist

Mark E. Bouska, PMP

Jean M. Kelm, PMP, CAMS

Nanette S. Patton, MSBA, PMP

Allan Shechet, MAOD, PMP

Renee Taylor, PMP

X2.9.2.2   Other Contributors

Nada Abandah

Srinivas Adusumilli, PMP

Panayotis Agrapidis, MSc Ceng

Hussain Ali Al-Ansari, EurIng, CEng

Fathalla M. Al-Hanbali, PMP

Mohammed Abdulla Al-Kuwari, EurIng, PMP

Rania Al-Maghraby, MSc, PMP

Guna Appalaraju

Jennifer A. Arndt, PMP, PgMP

Mario Arlt, PMP

Raviendran Arunasalem, PMP

Robert F. Babb II, PMP, PhD

Dennis G. Ballow, Sr., PMP, MAEd

Dimah M. Barakat, PMP

Nathaniel Barksdale, Jr., PhD, PMP
Daniel J. Barnardo
Kenneth J. Barry
Mohammed Safi Batley, MIM
John P. Benfield, PMP, SSBB
Murali K. Bharat, PMP
Michael F. Blankenstein, MS, PMP
Stephen F. Bonk, PE, PMP
Lynda Bourne, DPM, PMP
Eric D. Brown, MBA, PMP
Michael J. Browne, PhD, BSc
Jim Burkholder, PMP, CSSBB
Steve Buschle, PMP
John E. Buxton, PMP
Chris Cartwright, MPM, PMP
Kamaljeet K. Cato
Trevor Chappell, EurIng, FIET
Mubarak A. Chaudry
Noman Zafar Chaudry, PE, PMP
Rajasekhar Chevvuri, PMP
Reha Cimen, MBA, PMP
Daniel R. Crissman, MBA
Anthony J Cunningham, MSIS, PMP
William H. Dannenmaier, MBA, PMP
Allan Edward Dean, MBA, PMP
Jean-Michel De Jaeger, EMBA, PMP
Elizabeth Borges, PMP
Natalia Dimu, PMP
Karen K. Dunlap, PMP, SSGB
Hassan El-Meligy
Michael D. Farley, MBA, PMP
Joseph Fehrenbach, MBA, PMP
Paulo A. Ferreira, PMP
Claudio Fernando Freita
Steve Garfein, MBA, PMP
Stanisław Gasik
Anton Dantrell Gates
Yohan Gaumont

Mohamed Gouda Gebriel
Peter Glynne, MPM
Robert Goodhand, PMP
Shyam Kumar Gopinathan Nair, PMP
Evgenii Gromakov, PhD
Marian "Sami" Hall, PMP
Sheriff Hashem
Sandra Herrmann
Hideyuki Hikida, PMP
Bernard Hill, PhD, PMP
Brigitte Hoffmann, MBA, PMP
Ruth Houser, PMP
Zulfiqar Hussain, PE, PMP
Brian Irwin, MSM, PMP
Leon Jackson Jr., PMP, FEA
Swatee Jain
Ramon Jimenez, PMP
Tony Johnson
Hemant Julka
Chin-Chi Kao
Paul Karlzen, JD, PMP
Tomer Keidar
Harlan G. Kennedy, PEng, PMP
Rameshchandra B. Ketharaju, CSQA
Thomas C. Keuten, PMP, OPM3-CC
Adil O. Khan, PMP
Khalid Ahmad Khan, PE, PMP
Daniel Kim
Sarma Kompalli, PMP
Henry Kondo, PMP, CISA
Sudeendra Koushik, PMP
Wendy Kraly, MBA, PMP
Meeta Kumar, MBA, PMP
Sanjeeva Kuma
Lisa J. LaBonte, PMP
Joe LaGrua, MIS, PMP
Rupendra Mohan Lahoti, PMP
Rosalie Lalena
Morgan J. Langley, PMP

Marcelo La Roza
Nealand M. Lewis, MBA, PMP
John Lissaman, BEng, PMP
Rodrigo Loureiro, PMP
Venu G Madduri, MBA, PMP
Vishal Maheshwari, MBA, PMP
Prashant Malviya, PMP
Narendra Marikale, PMP
Greg Martin, PhD, PMP
Steven B. Martin, PMP
Tim Massie, PgMP, PMP
Laura Mazzaferro, PMP
Graham McHardy
Charmaine McKernan
Richard J. Meertens, MBA, PMP
Pauline P. Meilleur
Yan Bello Méndez, PMP
Geeta Menon, PMP
Louis J. Mercken, PMI Fellow, PMP
Laura Metzger
Stalin Michael, MS, MBA
Myles D. Miller, MBA, PMP
Beverley Miranda, MBA, PMP
Carlos Morais, PMP
Lincoln Sant'Ana Morales, PMP
David Morgen, MBA, PMP
Laurence Moss
Belatchew (Abby) Nadew, PMP
Nanduri V. Rao, PMP
Carlos Naranjo, PMP
Elena Navas
Roger P. Neeland, PhD, PMP
Nyanisi Joseph Nhlapo
David R. Nunn, MBA, PMP
Edgar Méndez Ocádiz, PMP
Molli Ong
Rebecca S. Overcash, MBA, PMP
Sathyanarayanan Pandalai, PMP, CISA
Shiri R. Persaud, PMP
Heidi Brakke Peterson, PMP

X2

Tonya M. Peterson, MSPM, PMP
Crispin ("Kik") Piney, BSc, PMP
Hari Pisati, MBA, PMP
Tracy Poon, PMP, MBA
Joshua R. Poulson, PMP
Richard Price
Brian Pubrat, PMP
Renato Putini, MBA
Elena Ramírez Márquez
S. Ramani, PMP, PgMP
Saifur Rehman, PE, PMP
Jose Carlos Arce Rioboo, MBA, PMP
Marlene Derian Robertson, PMP
Cláudio Barbosa Rodrigues, PMP
Virginia Oliva Rodriguez
Bernard Roduit
Angela M. Ruthenberg, PMP
Ahmed Saleh Bahakim, PMP
Saleh Sailik, PMP, PMOC
Sharad Saxena, PMP
John Schuyler, PE, PMP

Neel Shah, BBA, MIB
Creg A. Schumann
Angela P. Scott, PMP
Paul E. Shaltry, PMP
Archana Sharma, MS, PMP
Dinesh Sharma, MBA, PMP
Prakash Ramesh Sharma, MBB, PMP
Kazuo Shimizu, PMP
Shekhar Singh, PMP
Vivek Sivakumar, CAPM
Ron Sklaver, PMP
Jen L. Skrabak, MBA, PMP
Lavine Oscene Small
Ulrich Spiehl, MBA
V.S.Srividhya, MCA, PMP
Juergen Sturany, PMP
Michal Szymaczek, PMP
Gangesh Thakur, CPIM, PMP
Julio Toro Silva, MBA, PMP
Joyce Statz, PhD, PMP
Lisa A. Taylor, MS, PMP

Fuminori Toyama
Biagio Tramontana, PMP
S. Tsaltas, MBI, MMath
Venu Uppalapati, PMP
Srikanth U.S., MS, PGCPM
Ali Vahedi, MSc, PMP
Thierry Verlynde, PMP
Aloysio Vianna da Silva
Marconi Fabio Vieira, PMP
Hao Wang, PhD, PMP
Tim Washington
Colin D. Watson, MIEE, PM
Patrick Weaver, PMP, FCIOB
Kevin R. Wegryn, PMP, CPM
Thomas Williamson, PMP, SCPM
George N. Wolbert, PMP
Lai Chi Wong, PMP
Joseph M. Zaccaria, PMP
Rafael Beteli Silva Zanon, PMP
Cristina Zerpa, MC, PMP
Richard Zoomer
Paula M. K. Zygielszyper, PMP

REFERENCES

[1] Project Management Institute. 2013. *A Guide to the Project Management Body of Knowledge (PMBOK® Guide)*—Fifth Edition. Newtown Square, PA: author.

[2] Project Management Institute. 2013. *The Standard for Program Management*—Third Edition. Newtown Square, PA: author.

[3] Project Management Institute. 2013. *Organizational Project Management Maturity Model (OPM3®)*—Third Edition. Newtown Square, PA: author.

R

GLOSSARY

Aligning Processes [Process Group]. A Process Group to optimize the portfolio and manage strategic change, supply and demand, portfolio value, portfolio information, and portfolio risks.

Authorization. The process of approving, funding, and communicating the authorization for initiating work on a component included in a "balanced portfolio."

Authorize Portfolio [Process]. Process of allocating resources to execute selected portfolio components and to formally communicate portfolio-balancing decisions.

Authorizing and Controlling Processes [Process Group]. A Process Group to authorize portfolio components and provide ongoing portfolio oversight.

Benefit Realization Analysis [Technique]. A technique to analyze portfolio component achievement of planned benefits.

Capability and Capacity Analysis [Technique]. A technique performed to understand the human, financial, and asset capacity and capability of the organization in order to select, fund, and execute portfolio components.

Categorization of Components [Technique]. A technique to group portfolio components based on criteria.

Category. A predetermined key description used to group potential and authorized components to facilitate further decision making. Categories are linked to components with a common set of strategic goals.

Communication Methods [Tool]. Tools that share and distribute information among portfolio stakeholders, such as email, video conferencing, web portals, etc.

Communication Requirements Analysis [Technique]. A technique to determine the information needs of portfolio stakeholders and define the information type and format for delivery to stakeholders.

Component [Portfolio]. A discrete element of a portfolio that is a program, project, or other work.

Component Proposal. A recommendation or plan, business case, or feasibility study, developed by stakeholders or sponsors, to introduce or change a portfolio component or components.

Cost/Benefit Analysis [Technique]. A technique that weighs expected costs against expected financial and nonfinancial benefits (value) to determine the best (according to relevant criteria) course of action.

Define Portfolio [Process]. Process of creating an up-to-date list of qualified components and organizing them into relevant business groups to which a common set of decision filters and criteria can be applied for evaluation, selection, prioritization, and balancing.

Define Portfolio Roadmap [Process]. Process of defining the high-level portfolio components, multi-year milestones, and interdependencies.

Defining Processes [Process Group]. A Process Group to develop the portfolio strategic plan, charter, and the portfolio management plan and to define the portfolio and portfolio roadmap.

Develop Portfolio Charter [Process]. Process of developing the Portfolio Charter to authorize the portfolio manager to develop portfolio management processes that supports the portfolio.

Develop Portfolio Communication Management Plan [Process]. Process of developing the portfolio communication management plan, a subsidiary plan of the portfolio management plan, including engaging stakeholders and analyzing how the information and communications needs of the portfolio stakeholders will be met.

Develop Portfolio Management Plan [Process]. Process of defining the overall portfolio management, including subsidiary plans for portfolio communication, performance, and risk.

Develop Portfolio Performance Plan [Process]. Process of developing the portfolio performance management plan, a subsidiary plan of the portfolio management plan, including how portfolio value is defined and optimized through portfolio component allocation, targets, and results.

Develop Portfolio Risk Management Plan [Process]. Process of developing the portfolio risk management plan, a subsidiary plan of the portfolio management plan, including methods for managing and reporting risks.

Develop Portfolio Strategic Plan [Process]. Process of analyzing and developing the portfolio strategic plan to determine how the organizational strategy and goals will be carried out through the portfolio management processes.

Elicitation Techniques [Technique]. Techniques to gather requirements for portfolio planning.

Enterprise Environmental Factors [Output/Input]. Conditions, not under the immediate control of the team, that influence, constrain, or direct the project, program, or portfolio.

Evaluation. The process of scoring specific potential components using key indicators and their related weighted criteria for comparison purpose for further decision making.

Gap Analysis [Technique]. A technique to evaluate the current portfolio mix of components and determine changes needed so components may be added, changed, or terminated to rebalance the portfolio.

Governance Decisions [Output/Input]. Portfolio governing body decisions based on portfolio performance, component proposals, and risks as well as capability and capacity of resources, funding allocations, and future investment requirements.

Governance Recommendations [Output/Input]. Portfolio governing body recommendations based on portfolio performance, component proposals, and risks as well as capability and capacity of resources, funding allocations, and future investment requirements.

Graphical Analytical Methods [Tool]. Tools such as risk versus return charts, histograms, pie charts, and other methods to visualize portfolio information.

Identification of Components [Technique]. A technique to identify the portfolio components from an inventory of work or proposed components based on prioritization, objectives, expected benefits, and performance criteria.

Integration of Portfolio Management Plans [Technique]. A technique to align subsidiary portfolio plans with the portfolio management plan to ensure consistency.

Interdependency Analysis [Technique]. A technique to identify dependencies between portfolios, portfolio components, or with external elements.

Inventory of Work [Output/Input]. A list of active work that may be potential portfolio components and a starting point to develop a portfolio.

Investment Choice Assessment [Technique]. Technique to align the portfolio based on new and changing strategic objectives, evaluate responses to threats and opportunities, and indicate portfolio investment gaps.

Key Criteria. Predetermined measures, values, or conditions used in a scoring model to measure alignment with strategic goals.

Key Descriptors. A set of characteristics used to categorize and document a portfolio component for further decision making.

Manage Portfolio Information [Process]. Process of collecting, distributing, and ensuring required information available to portfolio stakeholders in a timely manner.

Manage Portfolio Risks [Process]. Process of assessing and combining the probability of occurrence and impact of identified risks; numerically analyzing the overall effect of selected risks on the portfolio; and prioritizing risks for subsequent further analysis or action.

Manage Portfolio Value [Process]. Process of identifying and managing how organizational benefits and value are defined and optimized through portfolio component allocation, targets, and results.

Manage Strategic Change [Process]. Process of responding to changes in organizational strategy and environment to assess impacting the portfolio and enable changes, including rebalancing and other portfolio changes.

Manage Supply and Demand [Process]. Process of identifying financial, human, and other resource availability and capability requirements; mapping against organizational and portfolio constraints and demands; and allocating resources according to portfolio allocation decisions.

Modeling and Analysis Tools [Tool]. Tools to measure risk and include probability (likelihood) and impact (consequences).

New Component. A component that is being added to an existing project portfolio.

G

Optimize Portfolio [Process]. Process of assessing the portfolio components based on the organization's selection and ranking processes in order to create the component mix with the greatest potential to collectively support the organization's strategy and goals.

Organizational Governance. The process by which an organization directs and controls its operational and strategic activities, and by which the organization responds to the legitimate rights, expectations, and desires of its stakeholders.

Organizational Process Assets [Output/Input]. Plans, processes, policies, procedures, and knowledge bases specific to and used by the performing organization.

Organizational Strategy and Objectives [Output/Input]. An organizational document that contains the mission and vision statements as well as goals, objectives, and strategies intended to achieve the vision.

Phase Gate. A review at the end of a phase in which a decision is made to continue to the next phase, to continue with modification, or to end a project or program.

Planning Sessions [Technique]. A technique to structure collaboration for planning portfolio activities such as to define and manage risks.

Portfolio. Projects, programs, subportfolios, and operations managed as a group to achieve strategic objectives.

Portfolio Authorization [Technique]. A technique to formally authorize portfolio components, allocate funding, and assign resources.

Portfolio Balancing. The process of optimizing the mix of portfolio components to further the strategic objectives of the organization.

Portfolio Charter [Output/Input]. The document issued by the portfolio sponsor that formally authorizes the existence of a portfolio and provides the portfolio manager with the authority to apply portfolio resources to portfolio activities.

Portfolio Communication Management [Knowledge Area]. A Knowledge Area that includes the processes required to develop the portfolio communication management plan and manage portfolio information.

Portfolio Communication Management Plan. A subsidiary plan or component of the portfolio management plan that defines all communication needs, establishes communication requirements, specifies frequency, and identifies recipients for information associated with the portfolio management process.

Portfolio Component Reports [Output/Input]. Status reports from the portfolio's program and project managers.

Portfolio Governance Management [Knowledge Area]. A Knowledge Area that includes the processes to develop the portfolio management plan; define, optimize, and authorize the portfolio; and provide ongoing portfolio oversight.

Portfolio Management. The centralized management of one or more portfolios to achieve strategic objectives.

Portfolio Management Information System [Tool]. A tool, manual or automated, for information collection and distribution to support the portfolio management processes.

Portfolio Management Plan. A formal, approved document that defines how the portfolio will be executed, monitored, and controlled to meet organizational strategy and objectives.

Portfolio Organizational Structure Analysis [Technique]. A technique to determine the portfolio management organizational structure and determine roles and responsibilities.

Portfolio Performance Management [Knowledge Area]. A Knowledge Area that includes the processes to develop the portfolio performance management plan, manage supply and demand, and portfolio value.

Portfolio Performance Management Plan. A subsidiary plan or component of the portfolio management plan that describes performance measures, reporting (on scope, cost, schedule, and resources), resource optimization, and benefits realization.

Portfolio Periodic Reporting and Review. The process of reporting on the portfolio components as a whole using key indicators and reviewing the performance of the component mix by comparing actual with anticipated evolution, value, risk level, spending, and strategic alignment.

Portfolio Process Assets [Output/Input]. Portfolio plans, processes, policies, procedures, and knowledge bases used by the portfolio manager and stakeholders.

Portfolio Reports [Output/Input]. Reports that provide information on performance, risks, resources, and governance decisions.

Portfolio Review Meetings [Technique]. A technique used by portfolio governance bodies to review the portfolio status and to make portfolio decisions.

Portfolio Risk. An uncertain event, set of events, or conditions that, if they occur, have one or more effects, either positive or negative, on at least one strategic business objective of the portfolio.

Portfolio Risk Management Plan. A subsidiary plan or component of the portfolio management plan that describes how risk management activities will be structured and performed.

Portfolio Risk Management [Knowledge Area]. A Knowledge Area that includes the processes required to develop the portfolio risk management plan and manage portfolio risks.

Portfolio Roadmap. A document that provides the high-level strategic direction and portfolio information in a chronological fashion for portfolio management and ensures dependencies within the portfolio are established and evaluated.

Portfolio Strategic Plan. A formal, approved document that describes the portfolio vision, objectives, and goals to achieve organizational strategy and objectives.

Portfolio Strategic Management [Knowledge Area]. A Knowledge Area that includes the processes required to develop the portfolio strategic plan, portfolio charter, portfolio roadmap, and manage strategic change.

G

Prioritization Analysis [Technique]. A technique to compare and rank selected portfolio components, based on their evaluation scores and other management considerations, to ensure alignment with organizational strategy and objectives.

Probability and Impact Matrix. A grid for mapping the probability of each risk occurrence and its impact on project objectives if that risk occurs.

Program. A group of related projects, subprograms, and program activities that are managed in a coordinated way to obtain benefits not available from managing them individually.

Program Management. The application of knowledge, skills, tools, and techniques to a program to meet the program requirements and to obtain benefits and control not available by managing projects individually.

Project. A temporary endeavor undertaken to create a unique product, service, or result.

Project Management. The application of knowledge, skills, tools, and techniques to project activities to meet the project requirements.

Provide Portfolio Oversight [Process]. Process of providing governance in identifying, documenting, authorizing, and controlling changes to the project portfolio.

Quantitative and Qualitative Analysis [Technique]. Techniques that include analyses to optimize the portfolio, such as scenario analysis, probability analysis, and cost/benefit analysis.

Readiness Assessment [Tool]. A tool to assess stakeholders' willingness and ability to implement portfolio-related changes.

Rebalancing Assessments [Tool]. A tool to assess the portfolio and consider rebalancing portfolio components, resource requirements, and the portfolio budget to realign the portfolio risks.

Risk. An uncertain event or condition that, if it occurs, has a positive or negative effect on one or more project objectives.

Risk Acceptance. A risk response strategy whereby the project team decides to acknowledge the risk and not take any action unless the risk occurs.

Risk Avoidance. A risk response strategy whereby the project team acts to eliminate the threat or protect the project from its impact.

Risk Mitigation. A risk response strategy whereby the project team acts to reduce the probability of occurrence or impact of a threat.

Risk Reviews [Technique]. A technique to evaluate existing risks and identify new risks.

Risk Transference. A risk response strategy whereby the project team shifts the impact of a threat to a third party, together with ownership of the response.

Scenario Analysis [Technique]. A technique to evaluate scenarios in order to predict their effect on portfolio objectives.

Scoring Model. A set of weighted criteria and corresponding key indicators to measure and score components for comparison and prioritization purposes.

Stakeholder. An individual, group, or organization who may affect, be affected by, or perceive itself to be affected by a decision, activity, or outcome of a project, program, or portfolio.

Stakeholder Analysis [Technique]. A technique to identify stakeholders by individual or group and determine their concerns, interests, influence, expectations, and requirements.

Strategic Alignment Analysis [Technique]. A technique that focuses on new or changing strategic objectives and goals to determine portfolio gaps.

Strategic Change. Any change in the strategic intentions and plans of the organization that can impact the contents of component definition, categories, filters, key indicators, and other decision-making parameters used for portfolio management.

Strategic Plan. A high-level document that explains the organization's vision and mission, plus the approach that will be adopted to achieve this mission and vision, including the specific goals and objectives to be achieved during the period covered by the document.

Strategy and Objectives. The definition of an organization's intended achievements in terms of business results interpreted from various perspectives—financial, customer, infrastructure, products and services, or by cultural outcomes that are measurable.

Subportfolio. A collection of components which includes programs, projects, portfolios, and other work grouped together within a larger portfolio.

Weighted Ranking and Scoring Techniques [Technique]. Techniques using a multiplication factor to rank and score portfolio components to convey the importance of criteria used.

G

INDEX

A

Aligning Process Group, 32
    processes
        manage portfolio information, 114–118
        manage portfolio risks, 129–135
        manage portfolio value, 96–104
        manage strategic change, 52–55
        manage supply and demand, 92–96
        optimize portfolio, 72–77
Assessment
    activities, 23
    results, 23–24
Authorize Portfolio
    data flow, 78
    description, 77–78
    inputs
        portfolio, 79
        portfolio management plan, 79
        portfolio reports, 79
    outputs
        portfolio management plan updates, 80
        portfolio process asset updates, 80
        portfolio reports, 80
        portfolio updates, 80
    tools and techniques
        portfolio authorization technique, 79
        portfolio management information system, 79
Authorizing Process Group, 32
    authorize portfolio, 77–80
    provide portfolio oversight, 80–84

B

Body of Knowledge, 20
Business value, 10

D

Define Portfolio
    data flow, 65
    description, 64
    inputs
        portfolio, 66
        portfolio charter, 66
        portfolio management plan, 66
        portfolio process assets, 66
        portfolio roadmap, 66
        portfolio strategic plan, 65–66
    outputs
        portfolio management plan updates, 70
        portfolio roadmap updates, 70
        portfolio updates, 70
    tools and techniques
        description, 66–67
        portfolio component categorization techniques, 68
        portfolio component inventory, 67
        weighted ranking and scoring techniques, 68–69
Define Portfolio Roadmap
    data flow, 50
    description, 49
    inputs
        portfolio, 50
        portfolio charter, 49
        portfolio strategic plan, 49
    inputs, tools and techniques, and outputs, 49
    outputs, portfolio roadmap, 51
    tools and techniques
        cost-benefit analysis, 51
        interdependency analysis, 51
        prioritization analysis, 51
Defining Process Group, 31
    define portfolio, 64–70
    define portfolio roadmap, 49–51

S

Stakeholders, 26
Strategy
  management, processes, 41–55
  organizational
    description, 7–8
    portfolio management and, 7–9, 21–22

plan, developing, 41–46
portfolio aligned with, 3
Subportfolios, description of, 3

V

Vision, organizational alignment, 24